ARE YOU SMARTER THAN A 10 YEAR OLD?

ARE YOU SMARTER THAN A 10 YEAR OLD?

Foreword by

NOEL EDMONDS

First published in Great Britain in 2007 by
Virgin Books Ltd
Thames Wharf Studios
Rainville Road
London
W6 9HA

A catalogue record for this book is available from the British Library.

ISBN 978 0 7535 1373 6

The Random House Group Limited supports The Forest Stewardship
Council® (FSC®), the leading international forest-certification organisation.
Our books carrying the FSC label are printed on FSC®-certified paper.
FSC is the only forest-certification scheme supported by the leading
environmental organisations, including Greenpeace. Our
paper procurement policy can be found at
www.randomhouse.co.uk/environment

Typeset by Phoenix Photosetting, Chatham, Kent
Printed and bound in Great Britain by Clays Ltd, St Ives plc

3 5 7 9 10 8 6 4

SO, YOU THINK YOU'RE SMARTER THAN A 10 YEAR OLD?

It's time to dust off that old school tie and dig out those dog-eared exercise books, because I'm taking you back to the classroom to test your knowledge against the nation's 10 year olds.

Whether you were teacher's pet or the class clown, a swotty Susan or a naughty Nigel, now's your chance to prove your academic prowess and that exams *really* were harder in your day.

Right then: pens and paper at the ready, tuck in that shirt and pay attention at the back, because I'm about to explain the rules.

They're deceptively simple, of course. This book is made up of 41 rounds of questions. In each round, just answer the ten questions correctly in order. For an added element of difficulty, you could impose a thirty-second time limit on answering each question. The more questions you get right, the more prize money you amass, and answer all ten correctly and you'll have the chance to answer a final, big-money question. Get it right and you've won the top prize – quarter of a million pounds!

Of course, you won't *actually* win quarter of a million pounds. All that's at stake in this game is your reputation. Because, get that question, or any of the other questions, wrong, and not only do you win nothing, but you'll also be forced to confess the humiliating truth, that 'I am *not* smarter than a 10 year old.'

The questions are all based on subjects from the current school curriculum, and are grouped by age and subject, so you could be answering questions on anything from age six French to age ten maths. But they all have one thing in common – your average 10 year old should be able to answer all these questions correctly.

So you should sail through them, right?

Well, all I will say is, never underestimate the challenge. Your diminutive opponents might seem like a pushover, but I can tell you there are some smart 10 year olds out there. And don't forget, Mozart was composing symphonies by the age of ten, and Tatum O'Neal won an Oscar in her tenth year, so you could be up against some stiff competition.

How will you fare in this challenge? Will you get a gold star or a 'could do better'? There's only one way to find out . . .

Class dismissed.

Noel Edmonds

Round 1

£1,000   **AGE 6 MUSIC**

WHICH OF THESE INSTRUMENTS CAN PLAY LONG NOTES?

| 1) | WOODBLOCK | 2) | WHISTLE |
| 3) | DRUM | 4) | CASTANETS |

£2,000   **AGE 6 NATURAL SCIENCE**

WHICH OF THESE WOULD YOU DO TO KEEP FIT?

| 1) | GO FOR A JOG | 2) | WATCH TV |
| 3) | READ A BOOK | 4) | SEND A TEXT MESSAGE |

£5,000   **AGE 7 ENGLISH**

WHICH OF THE FOLLOWING WORDS DOES NOT RHYME WITH BED?

| 1) | SAID | 2) | HEAD |
| 3) | FED | 4) | BAD |

£10,000 **AGE 7 NATURAL SCIENCE**

IN THE UK, DURING WHICH SEASON DO LEAVES CHANGE COLOUR AND FALL OFF TREES?

| 1) SPRING | 2) SUMMER |
| 3) WINTER | 4) AUTUMN |

£25,000 **AGE 8 WORLD GEOGRAPHY**

THE ALPS ARE MOUNTAINS GOING ACROSS THE NORTH OF WHICH COUNTRY?

| 1) FRANCE | 2) INDIA |
| 3) NEPAL | 4) ITALY |

£50,000 **AGE 8 CITIZENSHIP**

FOR WHAT DOES THE 'A' IN A HOSPITAL'S 'A&E' DEPARTMENT STAND?

| 1) AMBULANCE | 2) ANTISEPTIC |
| 3) ANTIBIOTIC | 4) ACCIDENT |

£75,000 **AGE 9 FRENCH**

WHAT DO THE FRENCH CALL APPLES?

| 1) PATISSERIE | 2) FRITES |
| 3) POIS | 4) POMMES |

£100,000 — AGE 9 PHYSICAL SCIENCE

WHICH OF THESE IS NOT A BATTERY TYPE?

1) AAA
2) AA
3) A
4) D

£125,000 — AGE 10 RELIGION

UNDER WHICH TREE DID BUDDHA BECOME ENLIGHTENED WHILE MEDITATING?

1) BANYAN
2) BODHI
3) BIRCH
4) BEECH

£150,000 — AGE 10 MUSIC

MUSICAL NOTES ARE MADE UP USING HOW MANY LETTERS?

1) 8
2) 6
3) 7
4) 26

£250,000 — ENGLISH

WHICH OF THESE IS A TYPE OF STORY?

1) FAIRY TALE
2) DAIRY TALE
3) HAIRY TALE
4) MARY TALE

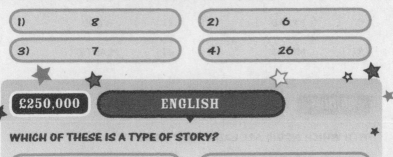

Congratulations: you are smarter than a ten-year-old!

Round 2

£1,000 — **AGE 6 CITIZENSHIP**

WHICH OF THESE ANIMALS IS NOT THE NAME OF A PEDESTRIAN CROSSING?

1) FLAMINGO
2) PELICAN
3) TOUCAN
4) ZEBRA

£2,000 — **AGE 6 FRENCH**

FROM WHAT IS A 'FRENCH STICK' MADE?

1) BREAD
2) WOOD
3) METAL
4) PLASTIC

£5,000 — **AGE 7 RELIGION**

WITH WHICH LIQUID ARE BABIES BAPTISED?

1) WINE
2) VINEGAR
3) MILK
4) WATER

SCORE

£10,000   **AGE 7 MUSIC**

IN THE CHILDREN'S SONG WHO WENT TO THE CUPBOARD TO FETCH A BONE FOR HER DOG?

1) OLD MACDONALD

2) LITTLE BOY BLUE

3) MARY MARY

4) OLD MOTHER HUBBARD

£25,000   **AGE 8 NATURAL SCIENCE**

WHICH OF THESE DO FISH NOT HAVE?

1) FINS

2) TAIL

3) FINGERS

4) SCALES

£50,000   **AGE 8 UK HISTORY**

WHO LIVED FIRST OUT OF THE FOLLOWING?

1) ISAMBARD KINGDOM BRUNEL

2) CHRISTOPHER COLUMBUS

3) THOMAS EDISON

4) FLORENCE NIGHTINGALE

£75,000   **AGE 9 WORLD GEOGRAPHY**

NEIL HAD NEVER HEARD OF LATVIA BEFORE HE WENT ON HOLIDAY BUT IN WHICH CONTINENT IS LATVIA?

1) ASIA

2) EUROPE

3) NORTH AMERICA

4) SOUTH AMERICA

£100,000 — AGE 9 PHYSICAL SCIENCE

WHICH OF THE FOLLOWING LIQUIDS WOULD YOU FIND IN A BATTERY?

1) OIL	2) COLA
3) ACID	4) SOUP

£125,000 — AGE 10 WORLD GEOGRAPHY

WHAT IS THE HIGHEST MOUNTAIN IN THE ANDES?

1) ACONCAGUA	2) K2
3) EVEREST	4) MONT BLANC

£150,000 — AGE 10 ENGLISH

WHICH BOOK LISTS WORDS WITH SIMILAR MEANINGS TO THE ONE FOR WHICH YOU ARE LOOKING?

1) ATLAS	2) THESAURUS
3) ENCYCLOPAEDIA	4) DICTIONARY

£250,000 — UK HISTORY

AT THE START OF WHICH CENTURY WAS QUEEN ELIZABETH II THE QUEEN OF ENGLAND?

1) 19th	2) 21st
3) 18th	4) 20th

Congratulations: you are smarter than a ten-year-old!

£1,000   **AGE 6 UK GEOGRAPHY**

WHAT IS THE CAPITAL OF WALES?

1) RHYL

2) SWANSEA

3) NEWPORT

4) CARDIFF

£2,000   **AGE 6 UK HISTORY**

WHICH WAS THE FIRST UK TV CHANNEL?

1) BBC 1

2) BBC 2

3) SKY ONE

4) MTV

£5,000   **AGE 7 ASTRONOMY**

HOW MANY LETTERS ARE THERE IN THE SHORTEST-NAMED PLANET OF OUR SOLAR SYSTEM?

1) FIVE

2) SIX

3) SEVEN

4) FOUR

£10,000 **AGE 7 PHYSICAL SCIENCE**

WHAT MAKES A SAIL WORK?

1) WIND

2) WAVES

3) FUEL

4) FIRE

£25,000 **AGE 8 UK GEOGRAPHY**

WHAT IS THE ORDNANCE SURVEY FAMOUS FOR PRODUCING?

1) MARKET RESEARCH

2) CARS

3) BOXES

4) MAPS

£50,000 **AGE 8 RELIGION**

IN WHICH CITY DOES THE POPE LIVE?

1) NEW YORK

2) LONDON

3) VATICAN CITY

4) PARIS

£75,000 **AGE 9 MUSIC**

A MINIM IS EQUAL TO HOW MANY BEATS?

1) 1/2

2) 2

3) 1

4) 4

£100,000 AGE 9 WORLD HISTORY

IN WHICH YEAR DID WORLD WAR II END?

1) 1935

2) 1945

3) 1939

4) 1949

£125,000 AGE 10 CITIZENSHIP

WHO SUCCEEDED GORDON BROWN AS CHANCELLOR?

1) ALISTAIR DARLING

2) RUTH KELLY

3) ED BALLS

4) DAVID MILIBAND

£150,000 AGE 10 RELIGION

WHICH OF THESE IS THE YOUNGEST OF THE WORLD'S RELIGIONS?

1) SIKHISM

2) BUDDHISM

3) JUDAISM

4) ISLAM

£250,000 ASTRONOMY

IF JOHNNY WAS WALKING IN THE MORNING AND THE SUN ROSE BEHIND HIM, WHICH DIRECTION WOULD HE BE WALKING?

1) WEST

2) EAST

3) NORTH

4) SOUTH

Congratulations: you are smarter than a ten-year-old!

£1,000 **AGE 6 UK GEOGRAPHY**

WHICH UK SEASIDE TOWN HAS A FAMOUS TOWER?

1) BLACKPOOL	2) SKEGNESS
3) BARMOUTH	4) SOUTHAMPTON

£2,000 **AGE 6 PHYSICAL SCIENCE**

WHICH OF THESE ITEMS WILL NOT FLOAT ON WATER?

1) WOOD	2) PAPER
3) CORK	4) BRASS

£5,000 **AGE 7 UK HISTORY**

FOR WHICH EMPIRE WAS HADRIAN A RULER?

1) OTTOMAN	2) ROMAN
3) KLINGON	4) GREEK

£10,000 — AGE 7 RELIGION

WHAT IS THE NAME GIVEN TO PEOPLE WHO FOLLOW THE ISLAMIC RELIGION?

1) CHRISTIANS
2) SIKHS
3) JEWS
4) MUSLIMS

£25,000 — AGE 8 MATHS

WHAT IS 6 SQUARED?

1) 8
2) 4
3) 25
4) 36

£50,000 — AGE 8 PHYSICAL SCIENCE

FROM WHERE DOES METAL COME?

1) THE SKY
2) THE SUN
3) FOSSILS
4) ORE

£75,000 — AGE 9 ASTRONOMY

WHAT WAS ASTRONAUT EDWIN ALDRIN'S NICKNAME?

1) CLAP
2) QUACK
3) BUZZ
4) HISS

£100,000   AGE 9 UK GEOGRAPHY

WHICH ISLAND HAS THE CAPITAL CALLED NEWPORT?

| 1) ISLE OF MAN | 2) SARK |
| 3) ISLE OF WIGHT | 4) SKYE |

£125,000   AGE 10 PHYSICAL SCIENCE

WHICH IS THE ONLY ROCK THAT FLOATS?

| 1) PUMICE | 2) MARBLE |
| 3) OBSIDIAN | 4) QUARTZ |

£150,000   AGE 10 CITIZENSHIP

WHICH OF THESE WAS NOT A PRIME MINISTER OF ENGLAND?

| 1) MARGARET THATCHER | 2) SIR MENZIES CAMPBELL |
| 3) TONY BLAIR | 4) HAROLD WILSON |

£250,000   ASTRONOMY

WHICH PLANET IS SOMETIMES CALLED THE THIRD ROCK FROM THE SUN?

| 1) EARTH | 2) VENUS |
| 3) MARS | 4) NEPTUNE |

Congratulations: you are smarter than a ten-year-old!

Round 5

£1,000 **AGE 6 NATURAL SCIENCE**

WHICH OF THESE PETS DOES NOT NORMALLY HAVE FUR?

1) TORTOISE

2) CAT

3) DOG

4) RABBIT

£2,000 **AGE 6 MATHS**

HOW MANY SIDES DOES A PENTAGON HAVE?

1) 5

2) 6

3) 3

4) 8

£5,000 **AGE 7 WORLD GEOGRAPHY**

WHAT IS THE WORLD'S BIGGEST CONTINENT?

1) EUROPE

2) NORTH AMERICA

3) AFRICA

4) ASIA

£10,000 **AGE 7 UK GEOGRAPHY**

WHICH ENGLISH CITY HAS TWO FOOTBALL STADIUMS AT EITHER END OF STANLEY PARK?

1) LIVERPOOL

2) MANCHESTER

3) NEWCASTLE

4) DERBY

£25,000 **AGE 8 FRENCH**

IF YOU AGREED TO A RENDEZVOUS WITH SOMEONE, WHAT WOULD YOU DO?

1) FIGHT THEM

2) AVOID THEM

3) MEET THEM

4) PHONE THEM

£50,000 **AGE 8 RELIGION**

WHAT 'A' WERE THE TWELVE MEN JESUS CHOSE TO BE HIS SPECIAL HELPERS?

1) ACOLYTES

2) APPRENTICES

3) APPENDICES

4) APOSTLES

£75,000 **AGE 9 PHYSICAL SCIENCE**

HOW MANY COLOURS ARE THERE IN THE SPECTRUM?

1) 7

2) 9

3) 11

4) 5

£100,000 · AGE 9 ENGLISH

WHAT IS A WORD THAT JOINS TWO SENTENCES TOGETHER CALLED?

1)	CONJUNCTION	2)	CONVECTION
3)	CONTRADICTION	4)	CONVENTION

£125,000 · AGE 10 WORLD HISTORY

WHAT WAS THE NAME OF ELVIS PRESLEY'S HOUSE, WHICH BECAME A MUSEUM TO HIM?

1)	NEVERLAND	2)	GRACELAND
3)	WONDERLAND	4)	DISNEYLAND

£150,000 · AGE 10 UK HISTORY

WHICH COLOUR ROSE REPRESENTED THE HOUSE OF YORK?

1)	RED	2)	WHITE
3)	PINK	4)	YELLOW

£250,000 · WORLD HISTORY

WHAT IS THE SURNAME OF THE FAMOUS VENETIAN EXPLORER MARCO?

1)	TREBOR	2)	TICTAC
3)	POLO	4)	FOX

Congratulations: you are smarter than a ten-year-old!

Round 6

£1,000   AGE 6 UK GEOGRAPHY

IN WHICH COUNTRY WOULD YOU FIND DUNDEE?

1) ENGLAND

2) WALES

3) NORTHERN IRELAND

4) SCOTLAND

£2,000   AGE 6 WORLD HISTORY

IN WHICH COUNTRY DID THE FRENCH REVOLUTION TAKE PLACE?

1) FRENCH GUINEA

2) CANADA

3) CHAD

4) FRANCE

£5,000   AGE 7 MATHS

JESSICA LEAVES HOME AT 7:30 AND ARRIVES AT SCHOOL AT 8:15. HOW LONG DOES IT TAKE IN MINUTES?

1) 40

2) 50

3) 60

4) 45

£10,000 — AGE 7 CITIZENSHIP

WHAT SHOULD A WOMAN DO WHEN INTRODUCED TO THE QUEEN?

1) BOW	2) SNEEZE
3) CLOSE HER EYES	4) CURTSEY

£25,000 — AGE 8 NATURAL SCIENCE

OF WHAT ARE CANINE, MOLAR AND INCISOR EXAMPLES?

1) ANIMALS	2) MUSCLES
3) PLANTS	4) TEETH

£50,000 — AGE 8 WORLD HISTORY

AFTER WORLD WAR II, INTO WHICH PARTS WAS GERMANY DIVIDED?

1) NORTH AND SOUTH	2) UPPER AND LOWER
3) EAST AND WEST	4) NORTH AND WEST

£75,000 — AGE 9 ENGLISH

WHAT IS A WORD THAT REPLACES A NOUN CALLED?

1) VERB	2) ADVERB
3) PRONOUN	4) ADJECTIVE

TIMER ||||||||||||||||||||||||||||||||||||||||||||||||||||||

£100,000 — AGE 9 WORLD GEOGRAPHY

THE CANADIAN CITY MONTREAL IS NAMED AFTER WHAT?

1) A RIVER

2) A MOUNTAIN

3) A PERSON

4) A SEA

£125,000 — AGE 10 FRENCH

WHAT IS THE FRENCH WORD FOR CASTLE?

1) ROOK

2) CASTILLE

3) CHATEAU

4) CASTELLAN

£150,000 — AGE 10 WORLD GEOGRAPHY

CHRIST THE REDEEMER IS A STATUE OVERLOOKING WHICH CITY?

1) RIO DE JANEIRO

2) SAO PAULO

3) BUENOS AIRES

4) SHANGHAI

£250,000 — ENGLISH

IN THE ENGLISH LANGUAGE, APPROXIMATELY HOW MANY WORDS ARE THERE?

1) 250,000

2) 25,000

3) 2,500

4) 250

Congratulations: you are smarter than a ten-year-old!

Round 7

£1,000 — **AGE 6 MATHS**

MIKE'S BIRTHDAY IS THREE DAYS AFTER MONDAY. WHICH DAY DOES HIS BIRTHDAY FALL ON?

1) WEDNESDAY

2) SATURDAY

3) SUNDAY

4) THURSDAY

£2,000 — **AGE 6 CITIZENSHIP**

WHAT FORM OF TRANSPORT TRAVELS ON A RAILWAY LINE?

1) TRAIN

2) BUS

3) BARGE

4) TAXI

£5,000 — **AGE 7 MATHS**

WHAT DOES THE MATHEMATICAL SYMBOL 'X' MEAN?

1) ADD

2) DIVIDE

3) SUBTRACT

4) MULTIPLY

£10,000   **AGE 7 MUSIC**

WHICH OF THESE STRINGED INSTRUMENTS IS THE SMALLEST?

| 1) CELLO | 2) VIOLIN |
| 3) VIOLA | 4) DOUBLE BASS |

£25,000   **AGE 8 MATHS**

PETER WANTS TO FIND THE QUOTIENT OF TWO NUMBERS. HOW DOES HE DO THAT?

| 1) MULTIPLY THEM TOGETHER | 2) ADD THEM TOGETHER |
| 3) DIVIDE THEM | 4) DIVIDE BOTH BY TEN |

£50,000   **AGE 8 PHYSICAL SCIENCE**

WHICH OF THESE IS NOT A TYPE OF ROCK?

| 1) SPONGE | 2) IGNEOUS |
| 3) SEDIMENTARY | 4) METAMORPHIC |

£75,000   **AGE 9 UK GEOGRAPHY**

WHICH OF THESE IS LOCATED BY BEN NEVIS?

| 1) DUNDEE | 2) FORT WILLIAM |
| 3) ABERDEEN | 4) FALKIRK |

SCORE

£100,000   **AGE 9 MUSIC**

HAIRSPRAY, OLIVER AND MY FAIR LADY ARE ALL TYPES OF WHAT?

1) OPERA
2) JAZZ
3) BLUES
4) MUSICAL

£125,000   **AGE 10 UK GEOGRAPHY**

IN WHICH COUNTY IS THE RADIO TELESCOPE JODRELL BANK?

1) CHESHIRE
2) STAFFORDSHIRE
3) WILTSHIRE
4) SUFFOLK

£150,000   **AGE 10 FRENCH**

WHAT IS THE TRANSLATION OF 'HOUSE' INTO FRENCH?

1) MANSION
2) MAISON
3) CHATEAU
4) TERRACE

£250,000   **MATHS**

WHAT IS 57 ROUNDED TO THE NEAREST TEN?

1) 60
2) 40
3) 50
4) 7

Congratulations: you are smarter than a ten-year-old!

Round 8

£1,000   **AGE 6 PHYSICAL SCIENCE**

WHAT DO YOU NEED TO FORM THE SHADOW OF AN OBJECT?

1)	LIGHT	2)	DARK
3)	WATER	4)	WIND

£2,000   **AGE 6 UK GEOGRAPHY**

ANNE WENT TO VISIT LOCH NESS IN THE SUMMER. WHICH COUNTRY DID SHE GO TO?

1)	SCOTLAND	2)	ENGLAND
3)	WALES	4)	NORTHERN IRELAND

£5,000   **AGE 7 MATHS**

HOW MANY CENTIMETRES ARE THERE IN A METRE?

1)	1000	2)	500
3)	10	4)	100

£10,000 — **AGE 7 ASTRONOMY**

HENRY'S FAVOURITE PLANET HAS A BIG RED SPOT. WHICH PLANET IS IT?

1) SATURN

2) MARS

3) JUPITER

4) VENUS

£25,000 — **AGE 8 UK GEOGRAPHY**

RHIAN AND HER FRIENDS WENT TO ALTON TOWERS FOR A DAY OUT. WHICH COUNTY IS IT FOUND IN?

1) DERBYSHIRE

2) STAFFORDSHIRE

3) CHESHIRE

4) CORNWALL

£50,000 — **AGE 8 MUSIC**

WHICH OF THESE INSTRUMENTS WOULD YOU NEED A BOW TO PLAY?

1) FLUTE

2) CYMBAL

3) CORNET

4) CELLO

£75,000 — **AGE 9 RELIGION**

IN WHICH COLOUR SARI WOULD A HINDU WOMAN GET MARRIED?

1) WHITE

2) BLUE

3) RED

4) GREEN

£100,000   **AGE 9 UK GEOGRAPHY**

WHAT SYMBOL INDICATES A GOLF COURSE ON A MAP?

1) FLAG	2) TEE
3) BALL	4) CLUB

£125,000   **AGE 10 RELIGION**

WHICH OF THESE IS NOT A BOOK IN THE OLD TESTAMENT?

1) ACTS	2) GENESIS
3) EXODUS	4) KINGS I

£150,000   **AGE 10 ASTRONOMY**

KENNY'S DAD WATCHED THE FIRST SPACE SHUTTLE MISSION. WHICH YEAR WAS THAT?

1) 1971	2) 1991
3) 1981	4) 2001

£250,000   **UK HISTORY**

WITH WHICH OF THESE WOULD SAMUEL PEPYS HAVE WRITTEN?

1) QUILL	2) BALLPOINT PEN
3) FELT TIP	4) STRAW

Congratulations: you are smarter than a ten-year-old!

Round 9

£1,000 **AGE 6 MATHS**

IT IS A WHOLE YEAR TILL JESSICA'S NEXT BIRTHDAY. HOW MANY WEEKS IS THAT?

1)	14	2)	24
3)	60	4)	52

£2,000 **AGE 6 ASTRONOMY**

WHICH COUNTRY OWNS THE SPACE SHUTTLE?

1)	UNITED KINGDOM	2)	USA
3)	RUSSIA	4)	CHINA

£5,000 **AGE 7 RELIGION**

IN THE BOOK OF GENESIS, WHICH ANIMAL TOLD EVE TO DISOBEY GOD?

1)	RAT	2)	MOUSE
3)	SNAKE	4)	SPIDER

£10,000   AGE 7 WORLD HISTORY

WHAT WAS THE NAME OF POCAHONTAS' FATHER?

1) NECTOWANCE

2) TOMOCOMO

3) KOCOUM

4) POWHATAN

£25,000   AGE 8 NATURAL SCIENCE

WHICH OF THESE IS NOT NORMALLY KEPT AS A FAMILY PET?

1) RABBIT

2) SQUIRREL

3) GUINEA PIG

4) HAMSTER

£50,000   AGE 8 PHYSICAL SCIENCE

WHAT LIGHTS UP THE SKY DURING THE DAY?

1) MOON

2) VOLCANOES

3) SUN

4) REFLECTIONS FROM THE SEA

£75,000   AGE 9 ASTRONOMY

WHICH PLANET HAS A DIAMETER APPROXIMATELY 11 TIMES THE SIZE OF THE EARTH?

1) MARS

2) JUPITER

3) MERCURY

4) URANUS

£100,000 AGE 9 WORLD HISTORY

WHICH OF THESE HAPPENED FIRST?

1) WORLD WAR I

2) WARS OF THE ROSES

3) WORLD WAR II

4) CRIMEAN WAR

£125,000 AGE 10 MATHS

WHAT IS 0.4 AS A PERCENTAGE?

1) 40%

2) 10%

3) 200%

4) 2%

£150,000 AGE 10 UK GEOGRAPHY

ON WHICH RIVER IS CHESTER LOCATED?

1) TRENT

2) TYNE

3) TAY

4) DEE

£250,000 WORLD GEOGRAPHY

WHERE ARE YOU LIKELY TO MEET A ZULU?

1) AFRICA

2) EUROPE

3) ASIA

4) NORTH AMERICA

Congratulations: you are smarter than a ten-year-old!

Round 10

£1,000 **AGE 6 MUSIC**

COMPLETE THE TITLE OF THE CHRISTMAS CAROL, 'SILENT' WHAT?

1) DONKEY

2) BETHLEHEM

3) NIGHT

4) BABY

£2,000 **AGE 6 CITIZENSHIP**

WHICH COLOUR IS ASSOCIATED WITH ENVIRONMENTAL ISSUES?

1) BLUE

2) BLACK

3) YELLOW

4) GREEN

£5,000 **AGE 7 UK GEOGRAPHY**

WHAT IS THE LARGEST LAKE IN ENGLAND?

1) ULLSWATER

2) DERWENT WATER

3) LOCH NESS

4) WINDERMERE

£10,000 — AGE 7 NATURAL SCIENCE

BY WHAT NAME ARE A PERSON'S FIRST TEETH OFTEN CALLED?

1) COLA TEETH

2) WATER TEETH

3) MILK TEETH

4) SQUASH TEETH

£25,000 — AGE 8 UK GEOGRAPHY

JACK SAYS WHERE HE WENT AT THE WEEKEND HAD A MINSTER. WHERE DID HE GO?

1) MANCHESTER

2) GLASGOW

3) YORK

4) LIVERPOOL

£50,000 — AGE 8 NATURAL SCIENCE

WHICH GIRL'S NAME CAN ALSO MEAN A REEF WHERE SEA CREATURES LIVE?

1) CAROL

2) CLAIRE

3) CANDY

4) CORAL

£75,000 — AGE 9 CITIZENSHIP

WHICH OF THESE IS NOT A DAILY NEWSPAPER?

1) THE DAILY MAIL

2) THE DAILY BROADSHEET

3) THE DAILY EXPRESS

4) THE DAILY TELEGRAPH

£100,000 — AGE 9 ENGLISH

WHAT IS THE NAME GIVEN TO A WORD THAT CAN BE READ THE SAME FORWARDS AND BACKWARDS?

1) OXYMORON

2) ANAGRAM

3) ABBREVIATION

4) PALINDROME

£125,000 — AGE 10 MATHS

IF DECLAN BUYS A PAIR OF JEANS THAT SHOULD COST £40 BUT IN THE SALE HE GETS 10% OFF, WHAT IS THE NEW PRICE OF THE JEANS?

1) £44

2) £30

3) £32

4) £36

£150,000 — AGE 10 NATURAL SCIENCE

WHICH OF THESE FRUITS CAN BE ALLOWED TO MATURE AND BE USED AS A BATHROOM SPONGE?

1) LOOFAH

2) BANANA

3) ORANGE

4) ZUCCHINI

£250,000 — ENGLISH

WHICH OF THESE IS NOT A NOUN?

1) SONG

2) BOOK

3) MUSIC

4) SING

Congratulations: you are smarter than a ten-year-old!

Round 11

£1,000   AGE 6 CITIZENSHIP

WHAT MUST YOU USE ON YOUR BICYCLE AT NIGHT?

1) LIGHTS

2) HORN

3) BELL

4) SPEEDOMETER

£2,000   AGE 6 ASTRONOMY

WHICH OF THE FOLLOWING DOESN'T ORBIT THE SUN?

1) EARTH

2) JUPITER

3) MARS

4) MOON

£5,000   AGE 7 WORLD GEOGRAPHY

ANDY VISITED WHICH ITALIAN CITY TO SEE THE COLOSSEUM?

1) ROME

2) FLORENCE

3) VENICE

4) MADRID

£10,000   **AGE 7 ASTRONOMY**

WHICH PLANET LIES BETWEEN SATURN AND NEPTUNE?

1) JUPITER

2) MERCURY

3) MARS

4) URANUS

£25,000   **AGE 8 UK HISTORY**

WHAT IS THE NAME OF QUEEN ELIZABETH II'S DAUGHTER?

1) MARY

2) VICTORIA

3) ANNE

4) DIANA

£50,000   **AGE 8 NATURAL SCIENCE**

HOW OFTEN CAN A HONEYBEE STING A HUMAN?

1) ONCE ONLY

2) ONCE A DAY

3) AS OFTEN AS IT WANTS

4) IT HAS NO STING

£75,000   **AGE 9 CITIZENSHIP**

WHAT IS THE NAME GIVEN TO SPRAY-PAINTED SLOGANS ON WALLS?

1) GRAFFITI

2) TAPESTRY

3) MURALS

4) COLLAGE

£100,000 — AGE 9 NATURAL SCIENCE

HOW MANY CANINE TEETH DO ADULT HUMANS NORMALLY HAVE?

1) 6

2) 4

3) 8

4) 2

£125,000 — AGE 10 UK GEOGRAPHY

PORTSMOUTH AND SOUTHAMPTON ARE BOTH IN WHICH COUNTY?

1) HAMPSHIRE

2) DORSET

3) DEVON

4) LANCASHIRE

£150,000 — AGE 10 UK HISTORY

WHAT WAS PRISON REFORMER ELIZABETH FRY'S MAIDEN NAME?

1) GURNEY

2) GARDINER

3) GREENE

4) GARFIELD

£250,000 — FRENCH

WHAT DOES THE FRENCH WORD 'AIDE' MEAN?

1) COPY

2) CHEAT

3) SHOW

4) HELP

Congratulations: you are smarter than a ten-year-old!

Round 12

£1,000 — **AGE 6 WORLD GEOGRAPHY**

ROME IS THE CAPITAL OF WHICH COUNTRY?

1) ITALY

2) SPAIN

3) FRANCE

4) HUNGARY

£2,000 — **AGE 6 RELIGION**

IN THE BOOK OF GENESIS, WHICH FRUIT DID EVE OFFER ADAM?

1) ORANGE

2) BANANA

3) PEACH

4) APPLE

£5,000 — **AGE 7 WORLD HISTORY**

WHAT ARE IMPRINTS OF PLANTS AND ANIMALS IN ROCKS CALLED?

1) DINOSAURS

2) FOOTPRINTS

3) FOSSILS

4) AMMONITES

£10,000 · **AGE 7 RELIGION**

WHAT IS THE NAME OF THE CELEBRATION OF A JEWISH BOY REACHING THE AGE OF 13?

1)	BAT MITZVAH	2)	BRIT MILAH
3)	BAR MITZVAH	4)	BRIT MITZVAH

£25,000 · **AGE 8 ENGLISH**

HOW MANY VOWELS ARE THERE IN THE ENGLISH ALPHABET?

1)	3	2)	5
3)	1	4)	7

£50,000 · **AGE 8 ASTRONOMY**

HOW MANY LETTERS ARE THERE IN THE LONGEST-NAMED PLANET?

1)	6	2)	7
3)	8	4)	9

£75,000 · **AGE 9 ENGLISH**

WHAT IS THE TERM FOR COMPARING ONE THING TO ANOTHER?

1)	SYNONYM	2)	ANTONYM
3)	SIMILE	4)	ALLITERATION

TIMER ▮▮

£100,000 — AGE 9 FRENCH

IF YOU HAVE CAFÉ AU LAIT, WHAT WOULD YOU BE DRINKING?

1) WHITE COFFEE	2) BLACK COFFEE
3) WHITE TEA	4) BLACK TEA

£125,000 — AGE 10 PHYSICAL SCIENCE

HYDROGEN, HELIUM AND GOLD ARE THREE EXAMPLES OF WHAT?

1) ANIMALS	2) FLOWERS
3) GEMS	4) ELEMENTS

£150,000 — AGE 10 UK HISTORY

WHAT WAS THE NAME OF HENRY VIII'S ONLY SURVIVING SON?

1) EDWARD	2) HENRY
3) RICHARD	4) JOHN

£250,000 — WORLD HISTORY

WHICH OF THESE COUNTRIES' HISTORICAL PERIODS WERE CALLED DYNASTIES?

1) AUSTRALIA	2) SOUTH AFRICA
3) ARGENTINA	4) CHINA

Congratulations: you are smarter than a ten-year-old!

Round 13

£1,000   **AGE 6 MATHS**

HOW MANY DAYS ARE THERE IN A FORTNIGHT?

1) 7

2) 28

3) 14

4) 24

£2,000   **AGE 6 FRENCH**

WHICH OF THESE IS NOT A FRENCH CAR?

1) FERRARI

2) RENAULT

3) PEUGEOT

4) CITROEN

£5,000   **AGE 7 ASTRONOMY**

WHICH OF THE FOLLOWING PLANETS IS SMALLER THAN THE EARTH?

1) SATURN

2) JUPITER

3) NEPTUNE

4) MARS

£10,000 — AGE 7 CITIZENSHIP

IN MPH, WHAT IS THE NORMAL UK SPEED LIMIT IN BUILT-UP AREAS?

1) 40

2) 50

3) 30

4) 60

£25,000 — AGE 8 MATHS

KATIE HAD 54 SWEETS, SHE GAVE 11 TO HER FRIENDS BUT THEN RECEIVED 8 OTHERS FROM HER MUM. HOW MANY SWEETS HAS KATIE NOW?

1) 50

2) 52

3) 51

4) 41

£50,000 — AGE 8 CITIZENSHIP

WHERE WOULD YOU TAKE YOUR PET IF IT WAS ILL?

1) LIBRARY

2) VETERINARIAN

3) DOCTOR

4) HOSPITAL

£75,000 — AGE 9 WORLD GEOGRAPHY

WHICH AUSTRALIAN STATE IS THE LARGEST?

1) QUEENSLAND

2) WESTERN AUSTRALIA

3) NEW SOUTH WALES

4) VICTORIA

£100,000 — AGE 9 CITIZENSHIP

COUNTING AWAY FROM THE THUMB, ON WHICH FINGER IS A UK WEDDING RING WORN?

1) 1ST FINGER RIGHT HAND

2) 3RD FINGER LEFT HAND

3) 2ND FINGER LEFT HAND

4) 3RD FINGER RIGHT HAND

£125,000 — AGE 10 ENGLISH

WHAT IS A WORD CALLED IF IT SOUNDS THE SAME AS ANOTHER, BUT IS SPELLED DIFFERENTLY?

1) HOMOPHONE

2) GRAMOPHONE

3) TELEPHONE

4) METRONOME

£150,000 — AGE 10 MATHS

SUZIE HAS A BAG WITH 3 RED BALLS AND 1 WHITE BALL; IF SHE PULLS OUT ONE BALL, WHAT IS THE CHANCE IT WILL BE WHITE?

1) 25%

2) 50%

3) 75%

4) 67%

£250,000 — PHYSICAL SCIENCE

WHICH OF THESE NORMALLY MAKES A LIGHT BULB WORK?

1) OIL

2) PETROL

3) ELECTRICITY

4) WIND

Congratulations: you are smarter than a ten-year-old!

Round 14

£1,000   **AGE 6 ENGLISH**

WHICH TWO WORDS ARE OFTEN USED TO FINISH A STORY?

1) GOODBYE ALL

2) NO MORE

3) TURN OVER

4) THE END

£2,000   **AGE 6 MUSIC**

WHAT ARE BELLS MADE FROM?

1) WOOD

2) PLASTIC

3) RUBBER

4) METAL

£5,000   **AGE 7 CITIZENSHIP**

BY UK LAW, WHICH OF THESE MUST EVERYONE IN A CAR WEAR?

1) SCARF

2) GLASSES

3) SEAT BELT

4) SHOES

£10,000 · **AGE 7 WORLD GEOGRAPHY**

WHICH COUNTRY IS SPLIT INTO A NORTH AND A SOUTH ISLAND?

1) PAKISTAN	2) SEYCHELLES
3) NEW ZEALAND	4) BORNEO

£25,000 · **AGE 8 CITIZENSHIP**

WHERE DO PEOPLE GO TO FACE A TRIAL?

1) PITCH	2) ARENA
3) COURT	4) STADIUM

£50,000 · **AGE 8 WORLD GEOGRAPHY**

WHICH OCEAN IS THE THIRD BIGGEST AND HAS ASIA TO ITS NORTH AND AFRICA TO ITS WEST?

1) INDIAN	2) ATLANTIC
3) PACIFIC	4) ANTARCTIC

£75,000 · **AGE 9 ENGLISH**

HOW MANY CONSONANTS ARE THERE IN THE ENGLISH ALPHABET?

1) 5	2) 21
3) 11	4) 33

£100,000 — AGE 9 NATURAL SCIENCE

WHAT TAKES BLOOD BACK TO THE HEART?

1) TAXIS

2) VEINS

3) ARTERIES

4) VENTRICLES

£125,000 — AGE 10 FRENCH

WHICH ENGLISH LETTER SOUNDS LIKE THE ENGLISH TRANSLATION OF THE FRENCH WORD 'VOUS'?

1) U

2) C

3) B

4) I

£150,000 — AGE 10 MUSIC

A LYRICIST OFTEN WRITES WHAT?

1) LYRICS

2) LIMERICKS

3) SCRIPT

4) DIALOGUE

£250,000 — ENGLISH

WHICH OF THESE COMES FIRST IN ALPHABETICAL ORDER?

1) SEAS

2) SEAM

3) SEAT

4) SEAL

Congratulations: you are smarter than a ten-year-old!

Round 15

£1,000　　**AGE 6 RELIGION**

WHAT WAS THE NAME OF JESUS' MOTHER?

| 1) | CAROL | 2) | EVE |
| 3) | RUTH | 4) | MARY |

£2,000　　**AGE 6 PHYSICAL SCIENCE**

WHAT IS FROZEN WATER CALLED?

| 1) | STEAM | 2) | FOAM |
| 3) | ALCOHOL | 4) | ICE |

£5,000　　**AGE 7 UK GEOGRAPHY**

ON WHICH COAST WOULD YOU FIND BLACKPOOL?

| 1) | EAST | 2) | SOUTH |
| 3) | WEST | 4) | NORTH |

£10,000   AGE 7 UK HISTORY

APART FROM LEMON AND WATER, WHAT WOULD YOU NEED TO MAKE VICTORIAN LEMONADE?

1) SALT

2) SUGAR

3) PEPPER

4) CARBON DIOXIDE

£25,000   AGE 8 MUSIC

HAYLEY WENT TO WATCH A TRIO PLAY IN CONCERT. HOW MANY PLAYERS WERE THERE?

1) 5

2) 3

3) 4

4) 2

£50,000   AGE 8 NATURAL SCIENCE

WHICH OF THESE DOES NOT CONTAIN FAT?

1) MEAT

2) CRISPS

3) APPLE

4) COOKING OIL

£75,000   AGE 9 PHYSICAL SCIENCE

WHICH OF THESE IS NOT A METAL?

1) ONYX

2) GOLD

3) SILVER

4) ALUMINIUM

£100,000 — AGE 9 RELIGION

WHICH LETTER DO YOU HAVE TO FOLLOW TO BECOME A SIKH; THE FIVE WHAT?

1) Ks
2) Js
3) Ls
4) Ms

£125,000 — AGE 10 PHYSICAL SCIENCE

TWO PARTS OF WHICH CHEMICAL WHEN MIXED WITH ONE PART OF OXYGEN MAKES WATER?

1) HYDROGEN
2) NITROGEN
3) KRYPTON
4) HELIUM

£150,000 — AGE 10 ASTRONOMY

EUGENE CERNAN WAS THE LAST MAN TO DO WHAT?

1) WALK ON THE MOON
2) FLY TO MARS
3) CAPTAIN THE SPACE SHUTTLE
4) SEE HALLEY'S COMET

£250,000 — UK GEOGRAPHY

IN WHICH CITY IS THE NATIONAL EXHIBITION CENTRE?

1) LIVERPOOL
2) MANCHESTER
3) LLANDUDNO
4) BIRMINGHAM

Congratulations: you are smarter than a ten-year-old!

Round 16

£1,000 **AGE 6 ASTRONOMY**

WHICH IS THE SMALLEST PLANET?

1) MARS
2) EARTH
3) VENUS
4) MERCURY

£2,000 **AGE 6 WORLD GEOGRAPHY**

THE STATUE OF LIBERTY IS LOCATED IN WHICH COUNTRY?

1) AUSTRALIA
2) ENGLAND
3) USA
4) FRANCE

£5,000 **AGE 7 ASTRONOMY**

WHICH TWO PLANETS ARE BETWEEN THE EARTH AND SATURN?

1) MARS AND VENUS
2) VENUS AND JUPITER
3) MARS AND JUPITER
4) NEPTUNE AND MERCURY

SCORE

£10,000   **AGE 7 WORLD GEOGRAPHY**

IN WHICH COUNTRY WOULD YOU FIND THE CITY OF BUENOS AIRES?

1) BRAZIL	2) MEXICO
3) ARGENTINA	4) NEPAL

£25,000   **AGE 8 UK GEOGRAPHY**

WHAT COULD BE BENS IN SCOTLAND AND SLIEVES IN NORTHERN IRELAND?

1) RIVERS	2) CITIES
3) MOUNTAINS	4) LIGHTHOUSES

£50,000   **AGE 8 MUSIC**

SOMEONE WHO PLAYS MUSIC IN FRONT OF AN AUDIENCE IS OFTEN CALLED WHAT?

1) COMPOSER	2) PAINTER
3) PERFORMER	4) SCULPTOR

£75,000   **AGE 9 MATHS**

HOW MANY DEGREES ARE THERE IN A HALF TURN?

1) 360	2) 180
3) 90	4) 270

£100,000 — AGE 9 WORLD GEOGRAPHY

IN WHICH COUNTRY IS TAIPEI?

| 1) MALAYSIA | 2) TAIWAN |
| 3) HONG KONG | 4) RUSSIA |

£125,000 — AGE 10 MATHS

WHAT IS THE SQUARE ROOT OF 121?

| 1) 7 | 2) 9 |
| 3) 6.5 | 4) 11 |

£150,000 — AGE 10 RELIGION

IN FRONT OF WHICH OBJECT IS AN ARTI CEREMONY CONDUCTED?

| 1) PILLAR | 2) FIRE |
| 3) STATUE | 4) WATERFALL |

£250,000 — UK HISTORY

WHICH OF THESE BUILDINGS IN NOT IN LONDON?

| 1) HOUSES OF PARLIAMENT | 2) BUCKINGHAM PALACE |
| 3) ROYAL ARMOURIES | 4) WEMBLEY STADIUM |

Congratulations: you are smarter than a ten-year-old!

Round 17

£1,000   **AGE 6 ASTRONOMY**

HOW MANY PLANETS BEGIN WITH THE LETTER 'M'?

1)   1

2)   0

3)   3

4)   2

£2,000   **AGE 6 UK HISTORY**

IN WHICH MONTH IS REMEMBRANCE DAY?

1)   DECEMBER

2)   OCTOBER

3)   SEPTEMBER

4)   NOVEMBER

£5,000   **AGE 7 NATURAL SCIENCE**

WHICH OF THESE IS NOT A BREED OF DOG?

1)   JACK RUSSELL

2)   GERMAN SHEPHERD

3)   BOXER

4)   SIAMESE

£10,000 **AGE 7 WORLD GEOGRAPHY**

WHICH COUNTRY HAS A GRAND CANYON CARVED BY THE COLORADO RIVER?

1) GERMANY

2) CHINA

3) USA

4) FRANCE

£25,000 **AGE 8 PHYSICAL SCIENCE**

WHAT IS THE FORCE THAT KEEPS THINGS ON THE EARTH?

1) GRAVY

2) GRAVE

3) GRAVITY

4) GRAVEL

£50,000 **AGE 8 WORLD GEOGRAPHY**

IN WHICH CITY IS THE CN TOWER?

1) NEW YORK

2) TORONTO

3) SYDNEY

4) LONDON

£75,000 **AGE 9 ASTRONOMY**

JACKIE SAYS HER FAVOURITE PLANET IS THE ONE NAMED AFTER THE ROMAN GODDESS OF LOVE. WHAT IS JACKIE'S FAVOURITE PLANET?

1) VENUS

2) MARS

3) JUPITER

4) SATURN

SCORE

£100,000   **AGE 9 PHYSICAL SCIENCE**

WHICH OF THESE IS NOT A MEASURE OF TEMPERATURE?

1) KELVIN
2) NEWTON
3) CELSIUS
4) FAHRENHEIT

£125,000   **AGE 10 ENGLISH**

WHAT IS THE DASH BETWEEN TWO WORDS CALLED?

1) SIPHON
2) SIMILE
3) METAPHOR
4) HYPHEN

£150,000   **AGE 10 PHYSICAL SCIENCE**

WHICH OF THESE METALS WOULD BE ATTRACTED TO A MAGNET?

1) ALUMINIUM
2) COPPER
3) BRONZE
4) IRON

£250,000   **ENGLISH**

WHICH OF THE FOLLOWING IS A VERB?

1) PLAYING
2) CAT
3) QUICKLY
4) SPEED

Congratulations: you are smarter than a ten-year-old!

Round 18

£1,000   **AGE 6 CITIZENSHIP**

WHICH OF THE FOLLOWING CAN BE RECYCLED?

1) PAPER

2) GLASS

3) METAL

4) ALL OF THEM

£2,000   **AGE 6 ENGLISH**

WHICH OF THESE WORDS IS NOT AN ENGLISH WORD?

1) ONE

2) EINE

3) NINE

4) FOUR

£5,000   **AGE 7 UK GEOGRAPHY**

LIVERPOOL IS CLOSEST TO WHICH SEA?

1) SOUTH CHINA

2) IRISH

3) CASPIAN

4) SCOTTISH

£10,000   **AGE 7 ENGLISH**

IF WORDS SOUND THE SAME, THEY ARE SAID TO WHAT?

1) COMPLEMENT

2) CONFUSE

3) RHYME

4) AGREE

£2 000   **AGE 8 UK HISTORY**

WHICH KING OF ENGLAND WAS KNOWN AS 'THE LIONHEART'?

1) JOHN

2) RICHARD I

3) EDWARD I

4) WILLIAM I

£50,000   **AGE 8 ENGLISH**

WHICH OF THE FOLLOWING IS NOT A NOUN?

1) BOX

2) HAPPY

3) CLOWN

4) TABLE

£7 000   **AGE 9 WORLD GEOGRAPHY**

IN WHICH CONTINENT ARE THE ATLAS MOUNTAINS?

1) AFRICA

2) SOUTH AMERICA

3) NORTH AMERICA

4) ASIA

£100,000   **AGE 9 CITIZENSHIP**

HUDDERSFIELD, IPSWICH AND NORTHAMPTON ARE ALL WHICH OF THESE?

1) TOWNS	2) CITIES
3) COUNTIES	4) COUNTRIES

£125,000   **AGE 10 WORLD HISTORY**

FROM WHICH NATIVE AMERICAN TRIBE DID POCAHONTAS COME?

1) NAVAJO	2) SIOUX
3) MOHICAN	4) ALGONGUIN

£150,000   **AGE 10 CITIZENSHIP**

WHAT IS THE AREA THAT AN MP REPRESENTS CALLED?

1) REGION	2) WAPENTAKE
3) COUNTY	4) CONSTITUENCY

£250,000   **ASTRONOMY**

WHAT IS THE RUSSIAN EQUIVALENT OF AN ASTRONAUT?

1) SPACENAUT	2) GALAXYNAUT
3) UNINAUT	4) COSMONAUT

Congratulations: you are smarter than a ten-year-old!

Round 19

£1,000   **AGE 6 FRENCH**

WHICH OF THESE COUNTRIES DOES NOT HAVE FRENCH AS AN OFFICIAL LANGUAGE?

1)	BELGIUM	2)	SWITZERLAND
3)	CANADA	4)	ENGLAND

£2,000   **AGE 6 WORLD GEOGRAPHY**

SERBIA AND ESTONIA ARE BOTH LOCATED IN WHICH CONTINENT?

1)	ASIA	2)	NORTH AMERICA
3)	AFRICA	4)	EUROPE

£5,000   **AGE 7 WORLD HISTORY**

HOW MANY WONDERS OF THE ANCIENT WORLD WERE THERE?

1)	5	2)	7
3)	3	4)	1

£10,000   AGE 7 CITIZENSHIP

WHAT SHAPE IS THE SYMBOL FOR RECYCLING?

1) SQUARE

2) CIRCULAR

3) TRIANGULAR

4) HEXAGONAL

£25,000   AGE 8 MATHS

TOMMY WANTS TO BAKE A CAKE. WHICH OF THESE UNITS WOULD HE USE TO MEASURE THE INGREDIENTS?

1) KILOMETRES

2) CENTIMETRES

3) GRAMS

4) MILES PER HOUR

£50,000   AGE 8 FRENCH

WHICH OF THESE IS NOT A FRENCH COLOUR?

1) ROUGE

2) YELLOW

3) VERT

4) BLEU

£75,000   AGE 9 NATURAL SCIENCE

WHAT FLOWER IS ALSO THE NAME GIVEN TO THE COLOUR OF THE HUMAN EYE?

1) ROSE

2) IRIS

3) POPPY

4) CARNATION

£100,000 AGE 9 MATHS

WHAT IS 1/6 OF 36 PEARS?

1) 4 ORANGES

2) 6 PEARS

3) 5 APPLES

4) 3 PEARS

£125,000 AGE 10 PHYSICAL SCIENCE

WHAT IS MEASURED IN DECIBELS?

1) LIGHT

2) ODOUR

3) WEIGHT

4) SOUND

£150,000 AGE 10 MATHS

WHAT IS 1/2 + 1/10?

1) 1/12

2) 2/20

3) 2/4

4) 6/10

£250,000 WORLD HISTORY

OF WHICH OF THESE COUNTRIES ARE ABORIGINES NATIVE?

1) SOUTH AFRICA

2) NEW ZEALAND

3) ARGENTINA

4) AUSTRALIA

Congratulations: you are smarter than a ten-year-old!

Round 20

£1,000 **AGE 6 UK GEOGRAPHY**

EUROPE AND ASIA ARE NAMES OF WHAT?

1) ISLANDS

2) CITIES

3) RIVERS

4) CONTINENTS

£2,000 **AGE 6 FRENCH**

IN FRENCH, WHICH ANIMAL IS CALLED A 'CHAT'?

1) DOG

2) COW

3) CAT

4) PIG

£5,000 **AGE 7 NATURAL SCIENCE**

WHICH 'L' DO WE USE TO BREATHE?

1) LIVER

2) LUNGS

3) LEGS

4) LIPS

£10,000 **AGE 7 WORLD HISTORY**

FROM WHAT WERE THE BOATS OF THE ANGLO-SAXONS MADE?

1) IRON

2) GOLD

3) WOOD

4) CLOTH

£25,000 **AGE 8 UK HISTORY**

WHAT WAS FORMER PRIME MINISTER MR BLAIR'S FIRST NAME?

1) JOHN

2) ANTHONY

3) ERIC

4) GORDON

£50,000 **AGE 8 UK GEOGRAPHY**

WHICH OF THE FOLLOWING IS THE MOST NORTHERLY?

1) STOKE-ON-TRENT

2) SUNDERLAND

3) SWANSEA

4) SOUTHAMPTON

£75,000 **AGE 9 WORLD GEOGRAPHY**

WHAT IS THE CAPITAL OF MEXICO?

1) TOLUCA

2) LEON

3) SAO PAULO

4) MEXICO CITY

£100,000 **AGE 9 NATURAL SCIENCE**

WHAT IS THE NAME GIVEN TO ANIMALS WITH A BACKBONE?

1) INVERTEBRATES

2) SHELLFISH

3) RUMINANT

4) VERTEBRATES

£125,000 **AGE 10 MATHS**

WHAT IS EIGHT FORTY P.M. WRITTEN IN DIGITAL TIME?

1) 20:40

2) 08:40

3) 20:07

4) 04:80

£150,000 **AGE 10 WORLD HISTORY**

IN WHICH CENTURY WAS AMERICA DISCOVERED BY CHRISTOPHER COLUMBUS?

1) 17th

2) 19th

3) 13th

4) 15th

£250,000 **UK GEOGRAPHY**

MATERIAL CARVED OUT BY THE WATER IN A RIVER IS KNOWN AS WHAT?

1) DRAINAGE

2) DELTA

3) EROSION

4) MOUTH

Congratulations: you are smarter than a ten-year-old!

Round 21

£1,000   AGE 6 MUSIC

WHICH OF THESE INSTRUMENTS WOULD YOU HIT?

1) MARACAS

2) BELLS

3) WOODBLOCK

4) RECORDER

£2,000   AGE 6 RELIGION

WHICH DAY OF THE WEEK IS THE CHRISTIAN HOLY DAY?

1) SATURDAY

2) MONDAY

3) FRIDAY

4) SUNDAY

£5,000   AGE 7 MUSIC

WHAT DOES A COMPOSER WRITE?

1) STORIES

2) MUSIC

3) POEMS

4) LYRICS

£10,000 — AGE 7 FRENCH

WHAT DO WE CALL 'PETITS POIS'?

1)	CARROTS	2)	LEEKS
3)	PEAS	4)	BRUSSEL SPROUTS

£25,000 — AGE 8 RELIGION

WHICH OF THESE IS A TYPE OF STORY THAT JESUS TOLD TO TEACH SPIRITUAL TRUTH?

1)	FABLE	2)	PARABLE
3)	LEGEND	4)	FAIRY TALE

£50,000 — AGE 8 CITIZENSHIP

WHAT IS THE NATIONAL PROCESS TO SELECT AN MP CALLED?

1)	NOMINATION	2)	ELECTION
3)	PROMOTION	4)	SELECTION

£75,000 — AGE 9 RELIGION

WHICH OF THE FOLLOWING WOULD YOU MOST ASSOCIATE WITH DIWALI?

1)	CAKE	2)	CROWN
3)	CANDLE	4)	COAT

£100,000 AGE 9 FRENCH

WHAT IS THE ENGLISH WORD FOR THE FRENCH 'AIL', A SMELLY BULB POPULAR IN FRENCH COOKING?

1) GARLIC

2) CARROT

3) LEEK

4) POTATO

£125,000 AGE 10 ENGLISH

WHAT TYPE OF PHRASE CONTAINS MORE THAN ONE WORD DOING THE JOB OF AN ADVERB?

1) PROSE

2) OXYMORON

3) VERBOSE

4) ADVERBIAL

£150,000 AGE 10 ASTRONOMY

WHICH CONSTELLATION IS NAMED AFTER A FLYING HORSE?

1) LEO

2) HYDRA

3) VELA

4) PEGASUS

£250,000 WORLD GEOGRAPHY

WHAT IS THE CAPITAL OF EGYPT?

1) CASABLANCA

2) JERUSALEM

3) GIZA

4) CAIRO

Congratulations: you are smarter than a ten-year-old!

Round 22

£1,000 **AGE 6 WORLD GEOGRAPHY**

IN WHICH COUNTRY IS DISNEYLAND PARIS?

1) ITALY

2) USA

3) FRANCE

4) JAPAN

£2,000 **AGE 6 UK GEOGRAPHY**

IN WHICH COUNTRY IS BEN NEVIS?

1) FRANCE

2) GERMANY

3) SCOTLAND

4) SPAIN

£5,000 **AGE 7 PHYSICAL SCIENCE**

WHICH OF THESE WOULD YOU ADD TO GRAVY GRANULES TO MAKE GRAVY?

1) MILK

2) WATER

3) ORANGE

4) LEMON

£10,000 **AGE 7 FRENCH**

WHICH OF THESE MEANS 'ME' IN FRENCH?

1) MON

2) MOI

3) MA

4) MU

£25,000 **AGE 8 MATHS**

ROSIE HAS 4 CATS, 3 DOGS AND 11 FISH. HOW MANY PETS DOES SHE HAVE ALTOGETHER?

1) 12

2) 18

3) 16

4) 20

£50,000 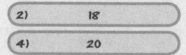 **AGE 8 PHYSICAL SCIENCE**

WHICH OF THESE IS NOT A SUSTAINABLE FUEL?

1) SOLAR

2) COAL

3) WAVE

4) WIND

£75,000 **AGE 9 WORLD HISTORY**

WHAT WAS THE SHORTENED NAME OF THE PARTY OF WHICH ADOLF HITLER WAS LEADER?

1) NAZI

2) GREEN

3) STASI

4) COMMUNIST

£100,000   AGE 9 ENGLISH

WHICH OF THESE LETTERS CAN SOMETIMES BE AN ENGLISH VOWEL?

1) Y

2) Q

3) K

4) Z

£125,000   AGE 10 MATHS

WHAT IS 0.3 DIVIDED BY 100?

1) 0.3

2) 3

3) 0.003

4) 30

£150,000   AGE 10 RELIGION

BETWEEN WHOM IS THE HINDU FESTIVAL OF RAKSHA BANDHAN CELEBRATED?

1) FATHER AND SON

2) MOTHER AND DAUGHTER

3) HUSBAND AND WIFE

4) BROTHER AND SISTER

£250,000   CITIZENSHIP

WHAT IS AN ORGANISATION CALLED THAT RAISES MONEY TO HELP OTHERS VIA DONATIONS?

1) SCHOOL

2) BANK

3) CHARITY

4) MICROWAVE

Congratulations: you are smarter than a ten-year-old!

Round 23

£1,000   **AGE 6 WORLD GEOGRAPHY**

THE GIRAFFE IS FROM WHICH COUNTRY?

1) INDIA

2) AUSTRALIA

3) AFRICA

4) SOUTH AFRICA

£2,000   **AGE 6 UK HISTORY**

WHICH OF THESE WAS NOT A QUEEN OF ENGLAND?

1) JANE

2) VICTORIA

3) MATILDA

4) ELIZABETH

£5,000   **AGE 7 FRENCH**

WHICH OF THESE IS FRENCH FOR WATER?

1) EAU

2) OWE

3) UH

4) HOE

£10,000 — **AGE 7 NATURAL SCIENCE**

WHICH OF THE FOLLOWING IS NOT A TREE?

1) OAK
2) IVY
3) ELM
4) ASH

£25,000 — **AGE 8 WORLD HISTORY**

IN WHICH WAR DID MARY SEACOLE BECOME FAMOUS?

1) CRIMEAN
2) WORLD WAR I
3) WORLD WAR II
4) BOER WAR

£50,000 — **AGE 8 MUSIC**

WHICH OF THESE IS A TYPE OF SAXOPHONE?

1) SPANISH
2) SHINY
3) ALTO
4) SALLY

£75,000 — **AGE 9 UK GEOGRAPHY**

WHAT DO CROSSED SWORDS ON A MAP INDICATE?

1) BATTLEFIELD
2) SWORD SHOP
3) TREASURE
4) HISTORICAL MONUMENT

£100,000 — AGE 9 MUSIC

WHICH OF THESE IS NOT A MUSICAL NOTE?

1) PAH
2) LAH
3) FAH
4) TE

£125,000 — AGE 10 PHYSICAL SCIENCE

WHICH OF THESE MUST AN ELECTRIC CIRCUIT HAVE FOR IT TO WORK?

1) BULB
2) METER
3) RESISTOR
4) BATTERY

£150,000 — AGE 10 ASTRONOMY

WHICH PLANET HAS THE SHORTEST DAY?

1) SATURN
2) EARTH
3) MERCURY
4) NEPTUNE

£250,000 — WORLD HISTORY

FOR WHAT DOES THE ABBREVIATION A.D. STAND?

1) AFTER DINNER
2) ALPHA DELTA
3) ANCIENT DATE
4) ANNO DOMINI

Congratulations: you are smarter than a ten-year-old!

Round 24

£1,000 | **AGE 6 RELIGION**

IN CHRISTIANITY, WHAT IS THE NAME OF THE FAMILY PRAYER THAT JESUS GAVE HIS FOLLOWERS?

1) THE TEN COMMANDMENTS

2) THE SERMON ON THE MOUNT

3) THE LORD'S PRAYER

4) THE LORD'S SUPPER

£2,000 | **AGE 6 PHYSICAL SCIENCE**

WHICH OF THE FOLLOWING IS WATERPROOF?

1) SPONGE

2) COTTON

3) WOOL

4) PLASTIC

£5,000 | **AGE 7 PHYSICAL SCIENCE**

WHICH IS THE HEAVIEST?

1) A BRICK

2) A FEATHER

3) A BAR OF SOAP

4) A GLASS OF WATER

£10,000 **AGE 7 UK HISTORY**

WHICH EMPIRE BUILT WALLS AROUND CITIES SUCH AS CHESTER AND YORK?

1) GREEK

2) ROMAN

3) ASSYRIAN

4) OTTOMAN

£25,000 **AGE 8 ENGLISH**

WHICH LETTER OF THE ALPHABET SOUNDS LIKE A QUESTION?

1) Y

2) D

3) G

4) T

£50,000 **AGE 8 WORLD GEOGRAPHY**

DANNY WENT ON A BOAT THROUGH BUDAPEST AND BRATISLAVA. WHICH RIVER WAS HE TRAVELLING ON?

1) TIBER

2) DANUBE

3) THAMES

4) LIFFEY

£75,000 **AGE 9 ASTRONOMY**

WHICH PLANET HAS MOONS NAMED AFTER CHARACTERS CREATED BY WILLIAM SHAKESPEARE AND ALEXANDER POPE?

1) URANUS

2) NEPTUNE

3) JUPITER

4) SATURN

£100,000 — AGE 9 RELIGION

BY WHAT NAME IS THE HINDU BELIEF OF CAUSE AND EFFECT KNOWN?

| 1) | CHAMELEON | 2) | KARMA |
| 3) | YIN AND YANG | 4) | ALPHA AND OMEGA |

£125,000 — AGE 10 NATURAL SCIENCE

WHICH OF THESE IS NOT A HERBIVORE?

| 1) | RABBIT | 2) | SHEEP |
| 3) | COW | 4) | FROG |

£150,000 — AGE 10 MUSIC

WHICH COMPOSER WROTE THE 'CARNIVAL OF THE ANIMALS'?

| 1) | HAYDN | 2) | HANDEL |
| 3) | SAINT-SAENS | 4) | MINOGUE |

£250,000 — ASTRONOMY

WHICH OF THESE IS A RADIO TELESCOPE IN CHESHIRE?

| 1) | HUBBLE TELESCOPE | 2) | MOUNT WILSON OBSERVATORY |
| 3) | HALE TELESCOPE | 4) | JODRELL BANK |

Congratulations: you are smarter than a ten-year-old!

Round 25

£1,000 — AGE 6 NATURAL SCIENCE

WHAT COLOUR STRIPES DOES A ZEBRA USUALLY HAVE?

1) BLACK AND YELLOW
2) GREY AND YELLOW
3) BLACK AND WHITE
4) BROWN AND YELLOW

£2,000 — AGE 6 UK HISTORY

HOW MANY KING HENRYS WERE THERE BEFORE QUEEN VICTORIA?

1) 10
2) 6
3) 8
4) 4

£5,000 — AGE 7 MUSIC

IN THE NURSERY RHYME 'TWINKLE TWINKLE LITTLE STAR' WHAT SHAPE IS THE STAR LIKE?

1) TRIANGLE
2) SQUARE
3) DIAMOND
4) CIRCLE

£10,000   **AGE 7 PHYSICAL SCIENCE**

WHICH COLOUR WOULD YOU GET IF YOU MIX BLACK AND WHITE?

1) BLUE	2) GREY
3) PINK	4) RED

£25,000   **AGE 8 WORLD HISTORY**

IN WHICH ITALIAN CITY DID WORK BEGIN ON A TOWER IN 1173 THAT WAS TO BECOME FAMOUS FOR LEANING?

1) PISA	2) ROME
3) NAPLES	4) VENICE

£50,000   **AGE 8 CITIZENSHIP**

IF SOMEONE IS SUSPECTED OF COMMITTING A CRIME, WHAT ARE THEY CALLED?

1) VICTIM	2) SUSPECT
3) GUILTY	4) CRIMINAL

£75,000   **AGE 9 MUSIC**

WHAT NOTE FOLLOWS ME, FAH, SOH?

1) LAH	2) SOH
3) TE	4) PO

£100,000   AGE 9 RELIGION

IN BUDDHISM, HOW MANY NOBLE TRUTHS ARE THERE?

1) 3	2) 2
3) 5	4) 4

£125,000   AGE 10 ENGLISH

WHICH IS THE SILENT LETTER IN THE WORD 'KNOW'?

1) N	2) O
3) W	4) K

£150,000   AGE 10 UK HISTORY

FROM WHICH KING DID OLIVER CROMWELL TAKE OVER?

1) RICHARD I	2) JOHN
3) EDWARD I	4) CHARLES I

£250,000   WORLD HISTORY

FROM WHICH OF THESE COUNTRIES DID THE ANGLO-SAXONS NOT COME?

1) GERMANY	2) DENMARK
3) SPAIN	4) HOLLAND

Congratulations: you are smarter than a ten-year-old!

£1,000   **AGE 6 PHYSICAL SCIENCE**

WHAT HAPPENS IF YOU PUT TWO IDENTICAL MAGNETIC POLES TOGETHER?

1) THEY ATTRACT

2) NOTHING

3) THEY REPEL

4) THEY DISINTEGRATE

£2,000   **AGE 6 NATURAL SCIENCE**

WHICH OF THE FOLLOWING NEVER CONTAINS MILK?

1) CHEESE

2) TOMATO KETCHUP

3) YOGHURT

4) CHOCOLATE

£5,000   **AGE 7 MATHS**

WHAT IS THE MATHEMATICAL SIGN FOR 'LESS THAN'?

1) >

2) <

3) £

4) %

£10,000 — AGE 7 UK GEOGRAPHY

WHICH OF THE FOLLOWING IS THE BIGGEST?

1) VILLAGE

2) CITY

3) TOWN

4) COUNTY

£25,000 — AGE 8 ASTRONOMY

IN WHICH DECADE DID EIGHT MEN WALK ON THE MOON?

1) 1960s

2) 1970s

3) 1980s

4) 1990s

£50,000 — AGE 8 NATURAL SCIENCE

WHICH OF THE FOLLOWING IS NOT A BONE IN THE HUMAN BODY?

1) TIBIA

2) RADIUS

3) BICEP

4) ULNA

£75,000 — AGE 9 UK GEOGRAPHY

WHICH OF THE FOLLOWING COULD YOU SEE IF YOU TRAVELLED ALONG THE RIVER THAMES ON A BOAT?

1) HOUSES OF PARLIAMENT

2) BLACKPOOL TOWER

3) THE ANGEL OF THE NORTH

4) EDEN PROJECT

£100,000 — AGE 9 UK HISTORY

WHICH TYPE OF ROOFS DID ANGLO-SAXON HOUSES HAVE?

1) THATCHED	2) TILED
3) SLATE	4) BRICK

£125,000 — AGE 10 FRENCH

WHICH OF THESE DOES 'TRES BIEN' MEAN?

1) OH DEAR	2) VERY GOOD
3) HELP ME	4) GO AWAY

£150,000 — AGE 10 ENGLISH

WHAT TERM IS APPLIED TO DESCRIBING SOMETHING AS SOMETHING ELSE?

1) POETRY	2) SYNONYM
3) METAPHOR	4) RHYME

£250,000 — WORLD HISTORY

IN WHICH COUNTRY DID THE BOSTON TEA PARTY TAKE PLACE?

1) CANADA	2) UNITED STATES
3) ENGLAND	4) WALES

Congratulations: you are smarter than a ten-year-old!

Round 27

£1,000 AGE 6 FRENCH

WHICH OF THESE IS THE FRENCH FOR 'JOHN'?

1) LUKE

2) PIERRE

3) JEAN

4) FRANCOIS

£2,000 AGE 6 ENGLISH

WHICH PUNCTUATION MARK IS USED AT THE END OF A NORMAL SENTENCE?

1) COMMA

2) ASTERISK

3) FULL STOP

4) HASH

£5,000 AGE 7 UK HISTORY

WHAT WAS HENRY VIII'S SURNAME?

1) PLANTAGENET

2) STUART

3) TUDOR

4) YORK

£10,000   **AGE 7 UK GEOGRAPHY**

WHICH OF THESE IS A RIVER IN SCOTLAND?

1) THAMES

2) TAY

3) TRENT

4) TAFF

£25,000   **AGE 8 WORLD GEOGRAPHY**

WHICH SEA SEPARATES NEW ZEALAND FROM AUSTRALIA?

1) TASMAN

2) QUEENSLAND

3) SYDNEY

4) AYERS

£50,000   **AGE 8 MUSIC**

WHICH OF THESE VOICES IS THE HIGHEST?

1) SOPRANO

2) BASS

3) ALTO

4) TENOR

£75,000   **AGE 9 UK HISTORY**

WHO RULED ENGLAND IMMEDIATELY BEFORE THE ANGLO-SAXONS?

1) ROMANS

2) GREEKS

3) FRENCH

4) AMERICANS

£100,000   **AGE 9 MATHS**

HOW MANY DEGREES ARE THERE IN A CIRCLE?

1) 90	2) 60
3) 180	4) 360

£125,000   **AGE 10 UK HISTORY**

WHAT WAS MONEY PAID TO A DEAD PERSON'S FAMILY BY THE MURDERER IN ANGLO-SAXON TIMES CALLED?

1) BLOOD MONEY	2) TITHE
3) WAR TAX	4) WERGILD

£150,000   **AGE 10 FRENCH**

WHAT DO THE FRENCH CALL THE ENGLISH CHANNEL?

1) L'EAU	2) LE CHANNEL
3) LA MER ANGLAISE	4) LA MANCHE

£250,000   **MATHS**

IF SOPHIE EATS 0.25 OF A PIZZA, WHAT FRACTION HAS SHE EATEN?

1) 7/5	2) 5/7
3) 1/4	4) 2/5

Congratulations: you are smarter than a ten-year-old!

Round 28

£1,000 | **AGE 6 WORLD GEOGRAPHY**

ANNA WENT TO A COUNTRY THAT IS FAMOUS FOR EATING SNAILS AND FROGS' LEGS. WHICH COUNTRY DID SHE GO TO?

1) BELGIUM

2) FRANCE

3) ITALY

4) SPAIN

£2,000 | **AGE 6 RELIGION**

OF WHICH RELIGION ARE METHODISTS, ROMAN CATHOLICS AND PROTESTANTS EXAMPLES?

1) JUDAISM

2) BUDDHISM

3) CHRISTIANITY

4) ISLAM

£5,000 | **AGE 7 NATURAL SCIENCE**

WHICH OF THESE IS NOT A JOINT IN THE HUMAN BODY?

1) ANKLE

2) THIGH

3) KNEE

4) ELBOW

£10,000 — AGE 7 MUSIC

A GLOCKENSPIEL IS MADE FROM WHICH MATERIAL?

1) WOOD	2) PLASTIC
3) RUBBER	4) METAL

£25,000 — AGE 8 ASTRONOMY

WHICH OF THESE WAS A SPACE MISSION?

1) MERCURY	2) KRYPTON
3) CARBON	4) ZINC

£50,000 — AGE 8 FRENCH

WHAT IS FRENCH FOR MAN?

1) FEMME	2) LEMON
3) HOMME	4) MANUEL

£75,000 — AGE 9 CITIZENSHIP

'MEALS ON' WHAT IS A SERVICE WHERE ELDERLY AND DISABLED PEOPLE ARE DELIVERED MEALS DAILY?

1) WHEELS	2) DEALS
3) HEALS	4) SEALS

£100,000 **AGE 9 UK HISTORY**

THE HOUSES OF YORK AND WHERE FOUGHT THE WAR OF THE ROSES?

1) CHESTER

2) TUDOR

3) LANCASTER

4) WINDSOR

£125,000 **AGE 10 UK GEOGRAPHY**

WHAT ARE THE BRECON BEACONS?

1) GROUP OF LIGHTHOUSES

2) SMALL VILLAGES

3) NATIONAL PARK

4) SMALL LAKE

£150,000 **AGE 10 WORLD HISTORY**

IF THE SIDE THE BRITISH WERE ON DURING WORLD WAR II WERE CALLED THE ALLIES, WHO WERE THEY FIGHTING?

1) PAX

2) TAXIS

3) AXIS

4) SAX

£250,000 **MATHS**

IF MATTHEW EATS 3/4 OF A CAKE, WHAT FRACTION OF THE CAKE IS LEFT?

1) 3/4

2) 1/4

3) 1/2

4) 4/5

Congratulations: you are smarter than a ten-year-old!

Round 29

£1,000 **AGE 6 NATURAL SCIENCE**

WHAT IS A BABY DOG CALLED?

1) KITTEN

2) PUPPY

3) CALF

4) LAMB

£2,000 **AGE 6 WORLD GEOGRAPHY**

IF JENNY BROUGHT YOU BACK A TOY KOALA FROM HER HOLIDAYS, WHERE WAS SHE MOST LIKELY TO HAVE BEEN?

1) CANADA

2) FRANCE

3) AUSTRALIA

4) USA

£5,000 **AGE 7 ENGLISH**

WHICH LETTER OF THE ALPHABET SOUNDS LIKE A SMALL OCEAN?

1) C

2) E

3) J

4) G

£10,000 AGE 7 CITIZENSHIP

WHICH OF THESE IS NOT THE VALUE OF A UK BANKNOTE?

1) £5

2) £10

3) £25

4) £20

£25,000 AGE 8 UK HISTORY

WHO IS THE PATRON SAINT OF SCOTLAND?

1) ANDREW

2) GEORGE

3) DAVID

4) PATRICK

£50,000 AGE 8 RELIGION

DURING WHICH MONTH IS THE JEWISH NEW YEAR CELEBRATED?

1) MARCH

2) SEPTEMBER

3) JANUARY

4) JUNE

£75,000 AGE 9 ASTRONOMY

WHICH OF THE FOLLOWING PLANETS HAS NO MOONS?

1) EARTH

2) NEPTUNE

3) VENUS

4) MARS

£100,000 — AGE 9 RELIGION

WHICH FLOWER, IN BUDDHISM, SYMBOLISES PURITY AND DIVINE BIRTH?

1) LILY
2) LOTUS
3) ROSE
4) DAFFODIL

£125,000 — AGE 10 NATURAL SCIENCE

WHICH OF THESE DOES A MOLLUSC USUALLY HAVE?

1) FEET
2) SHELL
3) WINGS
4) UDDERS

£150,000 — AGE 10 ASTRONOMY

MESSIER 31 IS THE NEAREST WHAT TO THE EARTH?

1) STAR
2) PLANET
3) GALAXY
4) BLACK HOLE

£250,000 — MUSIC

WHAT IS A MUSICAL TUNE ALSO CALLED?

1) OSTINATO
2) MELODY
3) SCALE
4) ARPEGGIO

Congratulations: you are smarter than a ten-year-old!

£1,000 AGE 6 MUSIC

IN THE SONG 'THE FARMER'S IN HIS DEN', WHAT DO THEY ALL PAT?

1) BONE

2) DOG

3) CHILD

4) WIFE

£2,000 AGE 6 WORLD HISTORY

WHAT DID THE *TITANIC* HIT, CAUSING IT TO SINK?

1) ANOTHER SHIP

2) A LIGHTHOUSE

3) AN ICEBERG

4) ROCKS

£5,000 AGE 7 FRENCH

WHICH VEGETABLES, THAT CAN MAKE YOU CRY, DO THE FRENCH CALL 'OIGNONS'?

1) LEEKS

2) PEPPERS

3) ARTICHOKES

4) ONIONS

£10,000 AGE 7 MUSIC

WHICH OF THESE PEOPLE WOULD YOU FIND IN AN ORCHESTRA?

1) SINGERS

2) RECORDER PLAYERS

3) VIOLINISTS

4) SCULTPORS

£25,000 AGE 8 FRENCH

WHAT WAS A FRENCH DEVICE FOR CHOPPING OFF HEADS?

1) CHOPPING BOARD

2) GUILLOTINE

3) CLAPPER BOARD

4) CINEMA

£50,000 AGE 8 MUSIC

THE MUSIC WORD 'DURATION' CAN ALSO BE DESCRIBED AS WHAT?

1) LONG AND SHORT

2) HIGH AND LOW

3) LOUD AND QUIET

4) FAST AND SLOW

£75,000 AGE 9 NATURAL SCIENCE

WHAT IS THE NAME OF A BADGER'S HOME?

1) STY

2) DEN

3) DAM

4) SETT

£100,000 — AGE 9 ENGLISH

WHAT ARE TWO OR MORE WORDS FOUND TOGETHER IN A SENTENCE THAT START WITH THE SAME LETTER CALLED?

1) POEM

2) RHYME

3) ONOMATOPOEIA

4) ALLITERATION

£125,000 — AGE 10 FRENCH

WHICH OF THESE IS THE TRANSLATION OF THE DESSERT CRÈME BRÛLÉE?

1) BLACK CAKE

2) BLUE CHEESE

3) BROWN COW

4) BURNED CREAM

£150,000 — AGE 10 RELIGION

OUTSIDE THE GATES OF WHICH CITY WAS JESUS CRUCIFIED?

1) JERUSALEM

2) NAZARETH

3) BETHLEHEM

4) GALILEE

£250,000 — UK HISTORY

WHAT IS THE NAME OF THE 10-YEARLY SURVEY IN THE UK TO FIND OUT ABOUT WHO LIVES THERE?

1) SPOT CHECK

2) STOP CHECK

3) CENSUS

4) CONSENSUS

Congratulations: you are smarter than a ten-year-old!

Round 31

£1,000   AGE 6 MATHS

MUM SAYS IT'S AN HOUR UNTIL TEATIME BUT HOW MANY MINUTES IS THAT?

1) 24

2) 12

3) 6

4) 60

£2,000   AGE 6 PHYSICAL SCIENCE

WHICH OF THESE NEEDS ELECTRICITY TO WORK?

1) MIRROR

2) MOP

3) CD PLAYER

4) TAP

£5,000   AGE 7 MUSIC

'FAST AND SLOW' IN MUSIC IS OFTEN CALLED WHAT?

1) TEMPO

2) PITCH

3) DURATION

4) STRUCTURE

£10,000 — AGE 7 FRENCH

WHICH NUMBER IS SPELLED THE SAME IN FRENCH AND ENGLISH?

1) ONE

2) NINE

3) SIX

4) TWELVE

£25,000 — AGE 8 MATHS

HEIDI HAS 35 SWEETS AND WANTS TO SHARE THEM BETWEEN 5 PEOPLE; HOW MANY DO THEY GET EACH?

1) 7

2) 8

3) 6

4) 5

£50,000 — AGE 8 FRENCH

WHAT IS THE ENGLISH TRANSLATION OF 'FROMAGE'?

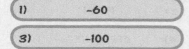

1) CREAM

2) MILK

3) CHEESE

4) YOGHURT

£75,000 — AGE 9 MATHS

WHICH OF THE FOLLOWING IS GREATER THAN –15?

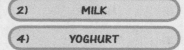

1) –60

2) –20

3) –100

4) –8

£100,000 — AGE 9 FRENCH

WHAT IS THE FRENCH WORD FOR CAKE?

1) GARÇON	2) CRÈME BRÛLÉE
3) CHAPEAU	4) GATEAU

£125,000 — AGE 10 MUSIC

GAMELAN MUSIC OFTEN USES A PENTATONIC SCALE BUT HOW MANY NOTES DOES THIS SCALE USE?

1) 6	2) 4
3) 5	4) 7

£150,000 — AGE 10 NATURAL SCIENCE

WHICH IS AT THE TOP OF THIS FOOD CHAIN?

1) GRASS	2) SNAKE
3) HAWK	4) GRASSHOPPER

£250,000 — RELIGION

WHICH OF THESE IS NOT A TRIBE OF ISRAEL?

1) LEVI	2) JUDAH
3) SAUL	4) REUBEN

Congratulations: you are smarter than a ten-year-old!

Round 32

£1,000 **AGE 6 RELIGION**

AS WHAT, IN CHRISTIANITY, ARE THE FATHER, THE SON AND THE HOLY GHOST KNOWN?

| 1) HOLY TRIANGLE | 2) HOLY TRINITY |
| 3) HOLY TRUMPET | 4) HOLY TINTAGEL |

£2,000 **AGE 6 WORLD HISTORY**

WHICH OF THESE IS NOT A TYPE OF GUN?

| 1) PISTOL | 2) MACHETE |
| 3) RIFLE | 4) REVOLVER |

£5,000 **AGE 7 UK HISTORY**

WHICH OF THESE WAS A FAMOUS QUEEN?

| 1) CLEOPATRA | 2) MARY MAGDALENE |
| 3) JOAN OF ARC | 4) MARY SEACOLE |

£10,000 — AGE 7 RELIGION

IN THE BIBLE, WHO SLEW GOLIATH WITH A STONE FROM A SLINGSHOT?

1) ABRAHAM	2) DAVID
3) SAMSON	4) MOSES

£25,000 — AGE 8 CITIZENSHIP

IN THE POLICE FORCE, WHICH OF THESE IS NOT A RANK?

1) SERGEANT	2) COLONEL
3) INSPECTOR	4) CONSTABLE

£50,000 — AGE 8 ASTRONOMY

DECLAN VISITED THE KENNEDY SPACE CENTER ON HIS HOLIDAYS. WHICH COUNTRY IS IT FOUND IN?

1) USA	2) CHINA
3) ENGLAND	4) FRANCE

£75,000 — AGE 9 FRENCH

WHICH OF THESE IS NOT A FRENCH WORD FOR 'THE'?

1) LES	2) LE
3) LA	4) LAS

£100,000 **AGE 9 UK GEOGRAPHY**

WHAT DOES A PINK TRIANGLE SIGNIFY ON A MAP?

| 1) VIEWPOINT | 2) TOWN HALL |
| 3) PICNIC SITE | 4) YOUTH HOSTEL |

£125,000 **AGE 10 NATURAL SCIENCE**

WHAT IS THE TERM FOR CHANGE OVER A LONG TIME MADE BY ANIMALS, ENABLING THEM TO SURVIVE?

| 1) REVOLUTION | 2) HERITAGE |
| 3) EVOLUTION | 4) ANCESTRY |

£150,000 **AGE 10 WORLD GEOGRAPHY**

ALPHABETICALLY WHICH WOULD BE FIRST IN A LIST OF CANADA'S PROVINCES?

| 1) BRISBANE | 2) ALBERTA |
| 3) ALASKA | 4) BRITISH COLUMBIA |

£250,000 **FRENCH**

IN WHICH OF THESE TV SHOWS DID TILLY SPEAK FRENCH?

| 1) TELETUBBIES | 2) TOTS TV |
| 3) ROSIE AND JIM | 4) MR BEAN |

Congratulations: you are smarter than a ten-year-old!

Round 33

£1,000   AGE 6 ENGLISH

IN THE ALPHABET, WHICH LETTER COMES JUST BEFORE 'N'?

1) M

2) L

3) O

4) P

£2,000   AGE 6 CITIZENSHIP

WHAT DO YOU PUT ON YOUR TOOTHBRUSH TO CLEAN YOUR TEETH?

1) SOAP

2) CHEESE

3) TOOTHPASTE

4) PAINT

£5,000   AGE 7 PHYSICAL SCIENCE

WHICH OF THESE IS THE MAIN PART OF THE AIR WE BREATHE?

1) HELIUM

2) HYDROGEN

3) CALCIUM

4) OXYGEN

£10,000 — AGE 7 CITIZENSHIP

WHEN RIDING A BICYCLE HOW SHOULD YOU INDICATE YOU WISH TO TURN RIGHT?

1) SHOUT 'I'M TURNING RIGHT'
2) PUT YOUR ARM OUT
3) PULL OUT
4) STICK YOUR LEG OUT

£25,000 — AGE 8 FRENCH

WHAT IS THE USUAL SHAPE FOR A CROISSANT?

1) SQUARE
2) CRESCENT
3) RECTANGULAR
4) TRIANGULAR

£50,000 — AGE 8 CITIZENSHIP

WITH WHICH OF THESE TWO DIGITS DO UK MOBILE PHONE NUMBERS START?

1) 07
2) 01
3) 09
4) 08

£75,000 — AGE 9 FRENCH

WHAT WOULD YOU DO WITH A FRENCH CHATEAU?

1) EAT IT
2) WEAR IT
3) THROW IT
4) LIVE IN IT

£100,000 AGE 9 NATURAL SCIENCE

WHAT PROTECTS THE HUMAN SPINAL CORD?

1) SKULL

2) RIBCAGE

3) BACKBONE

4) SHOULDER BLADES

£125,000 AGE 10 UK HISTORY

WHAT COMMON NAME WAS GIVEN TO THE RELIGIOUS GROUP OF WHICH PRISON REFORMER ELIZABETH FRY WAS A MEMBER?

1) METHODISTS

2) QUAKERS

3) CALVINISTS

4) MORMONS

£150,000 AGE 10 WORLD GEOGRAPHY

WHICH RIVER FLOWS OVER THE NIAGARA FALLS?

1) COLORADO

2) HUDSON

3) NIAGARA

4) MICHIGAN

£250,000 MUSIC

A TRIAD IS A CHORD WHICH CONTAINS HOW MANY NOTES?

1) 6

2) 3

3) 1

4) 2

Congratulations: you are smarter than a ten-year-old!

Round 34

£1,000 **AGE 6 MATHS**

JILL HAS 13 DOLLS AND BUYS 3 MORE. HOW MANY DOLLS DOES SHE HAVE NOW?

1) 10

2) 16

3) 133

4) 13

£2,000 **AGE 6 WORLD HISTORY**

WHICH TYPE OF BUILDINGS DID THE ANCIENT EGYPTIANS BUILD AS TOMBS FOR THEIR KINGS?

1) CUBES

2) PYRAMIDS

3) CREMATORIA

4) SHRINES

£5,000 **AGE 7 UK HISTORY**

WHICH OF THESE WAS BORN THE MOST RECENTLY?

1) FLORENCE NIGHTINGALE

2) POCAHONTAS

3) HENRY VIII

4) SAMUEL PEPYS

£10,000 **AGE 7 PHYSICAL SCIENCE**

WHICH OF THESE IS AN OBJECT THAT LIGHT CAN PASS THROUGH?

1) TRANSPARENT

2) IMPENETRABLE

3) OPAQUE

4) VEILED

£25,000 **AGE 8 ENGLISH**

WHICH OF THESE WORDS STARTS WITH A SOFT C?

1) CELERY

2) CAT

3) CANDLE

4) CLUE

£50,000 **AGE 8 RELIGION**

WHAT IS NORMALLY SAID BY MUSLIMS AFTER THE NAME OF MUHAMMAD?

1) PEACE ON EARTH

2) PEACE ON HIS HOLY NAME

3) PEACE BE UPON US

4) PEACE BE UPON HIM

£75,000 **AGE 9 PHYSICAL SCIENCE**

WHICH OF THE FOLLOWING IS NOT A PRIMARY COLOUR?

1) RED

2) YELLOW

3) BLUE

4) GREEN

£100,000   AGE 9 FRENCH

WHICH LETTER DO THE FRENCH ADD TO WORDS LIKE GATEAU AND CHATEAU TO PLURALISE THEM?

1) Y

2) S

3) Z

4) X

£125,000   AGE 10 CITIZENSHIP

WHAT IS THE FOURTH 'R' FOR SUSTAINABILITY: REDUCE, RECYCLE, REUSE AND WHAT?

1) RENOVATE

2) REFRESH

3) REPAIR

4) REDO

£150,000   AGE 10 ENGLISH

WHAT IS POETRY CALLED WHEN WORDS ARE WRITTEN TO FORM A SHAPE?

1) CLAY

2) CONCRETE

3) SLATE

4) MUD

£250,000   CITIZENSHIP

WHAT TYPE OF JACKET IS SOMETIMES USED ON A DANGEROUS CRIMINAL?

1) SMOKING JACKET

2) STRAITJACKET

3) LIFE JACKET

4) LEATHER JACKET

Congratulations: you are smarter than a ten-year-old!

Round 35

£1,000 **AGE 6 UK GEOGRAPHY**

A 'BIRD'S EYE' VIEW NORMALLY REFERS TO LOOKING AT SOMETHING FROM WHERE?

1) THE PAVEMENT

2) THE AIR

3) THE BIRD TABLE

4) THE CAR

£2,000 **AGE 6 RELIGION**

IN WHICH BUILDING DO MUSLIMS WORSHIP?

1) MOSQUE

2) CHAPEL

3) CATHEDRAL

4) CRYPT

£5,000 **AGE 7 ENGLISH**

IN WHICH ORDER ARE WORDS LISTED IN MOST DICTIONARIES?

1) ALPHABETICAL

2) SIZE

3) SOUND

4) POPULAR

£10,000   **AGE 7 RELIGION**

IN THE BIBLE, WHICH BOOK IS MADE UP OF POEMS?

1) NUMBERS	2) ACTS
3) PSALMS	4) REVELATION

£25,000   **AGE 8 FRENCH**

WHAT DOES 'PARLEZ-VOUS FRANÇAIS?' MEAN?

1) DO YOU SPEAK ENGLISH?	2) DO YOU SPEAK GERMAN?
3) DO YOU SPEAK ITALIAN?	4) DO YOU SPEAK FRENCH?

£50,000   **AGE 8 CITIZENSHIP**

WHICH OF THESE COULD YOU PUT ON A BUNCH OF KEYS TO HELP IDENTIFY THEM?

1) BOB	2) COB
3) JOB	4) FOB

£75,000   **AGE 9 PHYSICAL SCIENCE**

WHICH INSTRUMENT WOULD YOU USE TO OBSERVE THE STARS?

1) PERISCOPE	2) STETHOSCOPE
3) TELESCOPE	4) MICROSCOPE

£100,000 — AGE 9 NATURAL SCIENCE

WHAT IS THE NAME OF THE SMALL FUNGUS THAT IS USED TO MAKE BREAD RISE?

1) MUSHROOM

2) TOADSTOOL

3) TRUFFLE

4) YEAST

£125,000 — AGE 10 ASTRONOMY

HALLEY'S COMET WAS NAMED AFTER THE SURNAME OF AN ENGLISH ASTRONOMER, BUT WHAT WAS HIS FIRST NAME?

1) WILLIAM

2) GEORGE

3) EDMOND

4) ISAAC

£150,000 — AGE 10 UK GEOGRAPHY

WHICH OF THE FOLLOWING PLACES IS THE MOST SOUTHERLY?

1) CHESTER

2) CARLISLE

3) BRISTOL

4) SOUTHPORT

£250,000 — ASTRONOMY

WHAT WAS THE NAME OF THE FIRST DOG IN SPACE?

1) LAIKA

2) LUCKY

3) RANCA

4) BELKA

Congratulations: you are smarter than a ten-year-old!

Round 36

£1,000 — **AGE 6 WORLD HISTORY**

WHICH OF THE FOLLOWING WAS A POPULAR NAME FOR A FRENCH KING?

1) LIAM

2) LOUIS

3) LIONEL

4) LUKE

£2,000 — **AGE 6 FRENCH**

WHICH OF THESE GAMES IS DERIVED FROM A FRENCH WORD?

1) SQUASH

2) CROQUET

3) FOOTBALL

4) RUGBY

£5,000 — **AGE 7 WORLD GEOGRAPHY**

IN WHICH EUROPEAN COUNTRY IS MARSEILLE?

1) FRANCE

2) PORTUGAL

3) GERMANY

4) GREECE

£10,000 **AGE 7 MATHS**

WHAT NUMBER COMES NEXT IN THIS SEQUENCE? 4, 8, 12, 16 …

1) 21

2) 20

3) 19

4) 17

£25,000 **AGE 8 ASTRONOMY**

WHICH CONSTELLATION NAME MEANS A CRAB?

1) LEO

2) VIRGO

3) PISCES

4) CANCER

£50,000 **AGE 8 RELIGION**

WHAT IS THE NAME OF THE UNIVERSAL SOUL IN HINDUISM?

1) BRAHMAN

2) JESUS CHRIST

3) THE DALAI LAMA

4) MUHAMMAD

£75,000 **AGE 9 WORLD GEOGRAPHY**

WHICH AUSTRALIAN STATE STARTS WITH THE LETTER 'V'?

1) VALANCE

2) VICTORY

3) VANGUARD

4) VICTORIA

£100,000 — AGE 9 ASTRONOMY

A CLOCK USING THE SUN TO TELL THE TIME IS CALLED A SUN WHAT?

1) TIME

2) CLOCK

3) PREDICTOR

4) DIAL

£125,000 — AGE 10 WORLD GEOGRAPHY

WHICH IS THE LARGEST OF THE STATES OF AMERICA?

1) TEXAS

2) ALASKA

3) FLORIDA

4) MAINE

£150,000 — AGE 10 WORLD HISTORY

FROM WHICH COUNTRY DID NAPOLEON BONAPARTE COME?

1) GERMANY

2) FRANCE

3) ITALY

4) SPAIN

£250,000 — WORLD GEOGRAPHY

WHICH FRENCH CITY IS FAMOUS FOR ITS MUSTARD?

1) CANNES

2) DIJON

3) PARIS

4) TOULOUSE

Congratulations: you are smarter than a ten-year-old!

Round 37

£1,000   **AGE 6 MUSIC**

HOW MANY 'LITTLE SPECKLED FROGS SAT ON A SPLECKLED LOG'?

1)   10

2)   5

3)   4

4)   3

£2,000   **AGE 6 WORLD HISTORY**

OF WHICH COUNTRY WAS ADOLF HITLER LEADER?

1)   GERMANY

2)   ITALY

3)   AUSTRIA-HUNGARY

4)   SPAIN

£5,000   **AGE 7 ENGLISH**

WHAT IS THE PLURAL OF BOOK?

1)   BOOKES

2)   BOOK'S

3)   BOOKS

4)   BOOKSES

£10,000 **AGE 7 NATURAL SCIENCE**

WHAT IS THE NAME OF A BABY FROG?

1) TADPOLE

2) TOAD

3) NEWT

4) EFT

£25,000 **AGE 8 ENGLISH**

WHERE WOULD YOU FIND A SUFFIX?

1) END OF A WORD

2) START OF A WORD

3) MIDDLE OF A WORD

4) ON ITS OWN

£50,000 **AGE 8 ASTRONOMY**

BENNY SAID HE SAW A METEOR BUT JOHN SAID IT WAS CALLED SOMETHING ELSE. WHAT DID JOHN CALL IT?

1) SHOOTING STAR

2) CONSTELLATION

3) FLYING BOULDER

4) SPACESHIP

£75,000 **AGE 9 UK GEOGRAPHY**

WHAT IS THE HIGHEST MOUNTAIN IN NORTHERN IRELAND?

1) SLIEVE MUCK

2) SLIEVE MOUNTAIN

3) SLIEVE NEVIS

4) SLIEVE DONARD

£100,000   AGE 9 UK HISTORY

WHICH OF THE FOLLOWING WAS NOT AN ANGLO-SAXON KINGDOM?

1)	MERCIA	2)	NORTHUMBRIA
3)	CORNWALL	4)	WESSEX

£125,000   AGE 10 WORLD HISTORY

WHEN POCAHONTAS BECAME A CHRISTIAN, WHAT NAME DID SHE TAKE?

1)	MARY	2)	KYLIE
3)	REBECCA	4)	POLLY

£150,000   AGE 10 CITIZENSHIP

IF YOU RAISE A GLASS TO CELEBRATE SOMEONE, WHAT IS THIS CALLED?

1)	CEREAL	2)	FRY-UP
3)	TOAST	4)	SALUTE

£250,000   UK GEOGRAPHY

WHAT COLOUR ARE THE FAMOUS CLIFFS AT DOVER?

1)	RED	2)	WHITE
3)	BLACK	4)	BLUE

Congratulations: you are smarter than a ten-year-old!

£1,000 **AGE 6 UK HISTORY**

WHICH OF THESE IS NOT A PERIOD OF TIME IN ENGLAND'S HISTORY?

1) JASON

2) NORMAN

3) GEORGIAN

4) STUART

£2,000 **AGE 6 ENGLISH**

WHICH OF THE FOLLOWING WORDS RHYMES WITH 'HOUSE'?

1) CHOOSE

2) CRUISE

3) MOUSE

4) WHOSE

£5,000 **AGE 7 RELIGION**

AT SUNSET ON WHICH DAY DOES THE JEWISH SABBATH BEGIN?

1) FRIDAY

2) SATURDAY

3) SUNDAY

4) MONDAY

£10,000 — AGE 7 ASTRONOMY

WHICH OF THE FOLLOWING PLANETS IS BIGGER THAN THE EARTH?

1) NEPTUNE
2) MARS
3) MERCURY
4) VENUS

£25,000 — AGE 8 WORLD GEOGRAPHY

ANKARA IS THE CAPITAL OF WHICH COUNTRY?

1) TURKEY
2) CHINA
3) BULGARIA
4) SERBIA

£50,000 — AGE 8 WORLD HISTORY

FROM WHICH COUNTRY DID THE ROMANS COME?

1) ITALY
2) SPAIN
3) FRANCE
4) GERMANY

£75,000 — AGE 9 UK HISTORY

WHICH OF THESE TYPES OF BUILDINGS DID KING HENRY VIII DESTROY?

1) MONASTERIES
2) PALACES
3) CASTLES
4) PRISONS

£100,000 — AGE 9 MUSIC

WHICH IS THE CORRECT SPELLING OF A STRINGED INSTRUMENT FOUND IN AN ORCHESTRA?

1) CHELLO

2) CELO

3) CHALO

4) CELLO

£125,000 — AGE 10 WORLD HISTORY

WHAT DID GEORGE STEPHENSON INVENT FOR MINERS?

1) LIFT

2) SAFETY HELMET

3) PNEUMATIC DRILL

3) MINERS' LAMP

£150,000 — AGE 10 CITIZENSHIP

WHICH COLOUR ARE THE SEATS IN THE HOUSE OF LORDS?

1) GREEN

2) YELLOW

3) RED

4) BLUE

£250,000 — WORLD HISTORY

WHICH HULL MP LED THE PARLIAMENTARY CAMPAIGN AGAINST SLAVERY?

1) JOHN PRESCOTT

2) JOHN SMITH

3) WILLIAM WILBERFORCE

4) WINSTON CHURCHILL

Congratulations: you are smarter than a ten-year-old!

Round 39

£1,000   **AGE 6 NATURAL SCIENCE**

WHAT IS A BABY COW CALLED?

1)   PUP

2)   KITTEN

3)   CALF

4)   JOEY

£2,000   **AGE 6 MATHS**

HOW IS 5 HUNDREDS, 0 TENS AND 8 UNITS WRITTEN?

1)   580

2)   508

3)   850

4)   58

£5,000   **AGE 7 WORLD HISTORY**

HOW MANY WORLD WARS WERE THERE IN THE 20TH CENTURY?

1)   3

2)   2

3)   4

4)   1

£10,000 **AGE 7 MATHS**

WHAT IS THE TIME 6:45 IN WORDS?

1) QUARTER TO SEVEN

2) QUARTER PAST SEVEN

3) SIX O'CLOCK

4) FORTY-FIVE SEVEN

£25,000 **AGE 8 UK HISTORY**

WHAT IS THE NAME OF QUEEN ELIZABETH II'S HUSBAND?

1) ALBERT

2) CHARLES

3) EDWARD

4) PHILIP

£50,000 **AGE 8 RELIGION**

BY WHAT NAME IS THE 'FESTIVAL OF LIGHTS' KNOWN?

1) DIWALI

2) ONAM

3) NAVRATRI

4) PONGAL

£75,000 **AGE 9 MATHS**

WHAT IS THE AREA OF A SQUARE WITH SIDES OF 7CM?

1) 6 CM^2

2) 12 CM^2

3) 49 CM^2

4) 244 CM^2

£100,000 **AGE 9 WORLD HISTORY**

IN WHICH CENTURY WAS POCAHONTAS BORN?

1) 14th
2) 12th
3) 16th
4) 10th

£125,000 **AGE 10 UK HISTORY**

BY WHAT NAME WERE RICH ANGLO-SAXON FREEMEN KNOWN?

1) DUKES
2) EARLS
3) PRINCES
4) THANES

£150,000 **AGE 10 MUSIC**

A STEADY PULSE IN MUSIC CAN ALSO BE CALLED WHAT?

1) MELODY
2) BEAT
3) RHYTHM
4) TUNE

£250,000 **RELIGION**

WHAT IS A MANDIR?

1) TEMPLE
2) WAFER
3) PREACHER
4) SMALL CHURCH

Congratulations: you are smarter than a ten-year-old!

£1,000   **AGE 6 UK HISTORY**

WHICH FOOD IS NAMED AFTER THE EARL OF SANDWICH?

1) TOAST

2) SANDWICH

3) CAKE

4) LOAF

£2,000   **AGE 6 WORLD HISTORY**

ORIGINATING IN ANCIENT GREECE, WHAT IS A BUILDING WHERE BOOKS ARE LOANED OUT CALLED?

1) LIBRARY

2) HOSPITAL

3) YOUTH CLUB

4) CINEMA

£5,000   **AGE 7 WORLD HISTORY**

WHICH GREEK SPORT INVOLVED RACING A TYPE OF HORSE-DRAWN CART?

1) CARTOGRAPHY

2) HARNESS RACING

3) HORSE SLEDGING

4) CHARIOT RACING

£10,000 · AGE 7 PHYSICAL SCIENCE

WHAT SORT OF JACKET WOULD YOU WEAR AT SEA TO STOP YOU FROM DROWNING?

1) LIFE JACKET	2) SMOKING JACKET
3) TWEED JACKET	4) LEATHER JACKET

£25,000 · AGE 8 WORLD HISTORY

IN THE TRIANGULAR SLAVE TRADE, FROM WHICH CONTINENT WERE SLAVES TAKEN?

1) EUROPE	2) ASIA
3) SOUTH AMERICA	4) AFRICA

£50,000 · AGE 8 MATHS

JOHNNY HAS £1 AND SPENDS 52p ON SWEETS. HOW MUCH DOES HE HAVE LEFT?

1) 66p	2) 46p
3) 54p	4) 48p

£75,000 · AGE 9 MUSIC

WHICH OF THE FOLLOWING IS THE RECORDER THAT CAN PLAY THE HIGHEST NOTES?

1) TREBLE	2) DESCANT
3) SOPRANINO	4) BASS

TIMER ||||||||||||||||||||||||||||||||||||||||||||||||

£100,000 **AGE 9 WORLD HISTORY**

WHICH OF THESE LED ENGLAND TO VICTORY IN WORLD WAR II?

1) TONY BLAIR

2) WILLIAM PITT

3) WINSTON CHURCHILL

4) NEVILLE CHAMBERLAIN

£125,000 **AGE 10 PHYSICAL SCIENCE**

FOR WHAT DOES THE SYMBOL 'V' STAND IN ELECTRICAL MEASUREMENT TERMS?

1) VACUUM

2) VOLT

3) VOLCANO

4) VIDEO

£150,000 **AGE 10 NATURAL SCIENCE**

WHICH OF THE FOLLOWING IS NOT A PULSE?

1) PEA

2) BEAN

3) BANANA

4) LENTIL

£250,000 **WORLD GEOGRAPHY**

IN WHICH CITY WOULD YOU FIND THE SAGRADA FAMÍLIA CHURCH AND PARK GÜELL?

1) MADRID

2) BARCELONA

3) ROME

4) LISBON

Congratulations: you are smarter than a ten-year-old!

Round 41

£1,000   **AGE 6 CITIZENSHIP**

IN SIZE, WHICH OF THESE ENGLISH COINS IS THE SMALLEST?

1)   10p

2)   2p

3)   5p

4)   1p

£2,000   **AGE 6 ASTRONOMY**

WHICH PLANET IS THE COLDEST?

1)   MERCURY

2)   NEPTUNE

3)   EARTH

4)   SATURN

£5,000   **AGE 7 FRENCH**

WHAT WOULD YOU DO WITH FROMAGE FRAIS?

1)   EAT IT

2)   SIT ON IT

3)   READ IT

4)   WALK IT

TIMER |||||||||||||||||||||||||||||||||||||||||||||||||||||||

£10,000 — **AGE 7 WORLD HISTORY**

WHAT WAS THE SPANISH ARMADA?

1) FLEET OF SHIPS

2) SQUADRON OF AEROPLANES

3) COLUMN OF TANKS

4) CAVALRY UNIT

£25,000 — **AGE 8 MUSIC**

A MUSICAL SCALE IS MADE UP OF HOW MANY NOTES?

1) 9

2) 20

3) 3

4) 8

£50,000 — **AGE 8 WORLD HISTORY**

WHICH ENGLISH BANKNOTE SHOWED PRISON REFORMER
ELIZABETH FRY ON ITS REVERSE?

1) £10

2) £20

3) £50

4) £5

£75,000 — **AGE 9 CITIZENSHIP**

WHAT DO POLICE READ TO PEOPLE THEY ARREST?

1) THE BIBLE

2) THEIR RIGHTS

3) A NOVEL

4) THE HIGHWAY CODE

£100,000 — AGE 9 UK HISTORY

TO WHICH COUNTRY DID ENGLAND SEND PRISONERS DURING THE 1800s?

| 1) ARGENTINA | 2) AUSTRIA |
| 3) ARMENIA | 4) AUSTRALIA |

£125,000 — AGE 10 MUSIC

WHICH OF THE FOLLOWING IS NOT A FAMOUS COMPOSER?

| 1) BEETHOVEN | 2) PAVAROTTI |
| 3) SIBELIUS | 4) BRAHMS |

£150,000 — AGE 10 UK GEOGRAPHY

IN WHICH COUNTRY WOULD YOU FIND BOSTON?

| 1) SCOTLAND | 2) ENGLAND |
| 3) WALES | 4) NORTHERN IRELAND |

£250,000 — NATURAL SCIENCE

FROM WHICH CROP IS MOST FLOUR MADE?

| 1) OAT | 2) BARLEY |
| 3) WHEAT | 4) RICE |

Congratulations: you are smarter than a ten-year-old!

THE ANSWERS

Round 1

£1,000	WHISTLE
£2,000	GO FOR A JOG
£5,000	BAD
£10,000	AUTUMN
£25,000	ITALY
£50,000	ACCIDENT
£75,000	POMMES
£100,000	A
£125,000	BODHI
£150,000	7
£250,000	FAIRY TALE

Round 2

£1,000	FLAMINGO
£2,000	BREAD
£5,000	WATER
£10,000	OLD MOTHER HUBBARD
£25,000	FINGERS
£50,000	CHRISTOPHER COLUMBUS
£75,000	EUROPE
£100,000	ACID
£125,000	ACONCAGUA
£150,000	THESAURUS
£250,000	21st

Round 3

£1,000	CARDIFF
£2,000	BBC 1
£5,000	4
£10,000	WIND
£25,000	MAPS
£50,000	VATICAN CITY
£75,000	2
£100,000	1945
£125,000	ALISTAIR DARLING
£150,000	SIKHISM
£250,000	WEST

Round 4

£1,000	BLACKPOOL
£2,000	BRASS
£5,000	ROMAN
£10,000	MUSLIMS
£25,000	36
£50,000	ORE
£75,000	BUZZ
£100,000	ISLE OF WIGHT
£125,000	PUMICE
£150,000	SIR MENZIES CAMPBELL
£250,000	EARTH

Round 5

£1,000	TORTOISE
£2,000	5
£5,000	ASIA
£10,000	LIVERPOOL
£25,000	MEET THEM
£50,000	APOSTLES
£75,000	7
£100,000	CONJUNCTION
£125,000	GRACELAND
£150,000	WHITE
£250,000	POLO

Round 6

£1,000	SCOTLAND
£2,000	FRANCE
£5,000	45
£10,000	CURTSEY
£25,000	TEETH
£50,000	EAST AND WEST
£75,000	PRONOUN
£100,000	A MOUNTAIN
£125,000	CHATEAU
£150,000	RIO DE JANEIRO
£250,000	250,000

Round 7

£1,000	THURSDAY
£2,000	TRAIN
£5,000	MULTIPLY
£10,000	VIOLIN
£25,000	DIVIDE THEM
£50,000	SPONGE
£75,000	FORT WILLIAM
£100,000	MUSICALS
£125,000	CHESHIRE
£150,000	MAISON
£250,000	60

Round 8

£1,000	LIGHT
£2,000	SCOTLAND
£5,000	100
£10,000	JUPITER
£25,000	STAFFORDSHIRE
£50,000	CELLO
£75,000	RED
£100,000	FLAG
£125,000	ACTS
£150,000	1981
£250,000	QUILL

Round 9

£1,000	52
£2,000	USA
£5,000	SNAKE
£10,000	POWHATAN
£25,000	SQUIRREL
£50,000	SUN
£75,000	JUPITER
£100,000	WARS OF THE ROSES
£125,000	40%
£150,000	DEE
£250,000	AFRICA

Round 10

£1,000	NIGHT
£2,000	GREEN
£5,000	WINDERMERE
£10,000	MILK TEETH
£25,000	YORK
£50,000	CORAL
£75,000	THE DAILY BROADSHEET
£100,000	PALINDROME
£125,000	£36
£150,000	LOOFAH
£250,000	SING

Round 11

£1,000	LIGHTS
£2,000	MOON
£5,000	ROME
£10,000	URANUS
£25,000	ANNE
£50,000	ONCE ONLY
£75,000	GRAFFITI
£100,000	4
£125,000	HAMPSHIRE
£150,000	GURNEY
£250,000	HELP

Round 12

£1,000	ITALY
£2,000	APPLE
£5,000	FOSSILS
£10,000	BAR MITZVAH
£25,000	5
£50,000	7
£75,000	SIMILE
£100,000	WHITE COFFEE
£125,000	ELEMENTS
£150,000	EDWARD
£250,000	CHINA

Round 13

£1,000	14
£2,000	FERRARI
£5,000	MARS
£10,000	30
£25,000	51
£50,000	VETERINARIAN
£75,000	WESTERN AUSTRALIA
£100,000	3RD FINGER LEFT HAND
£125,000	HOMOPHONE
£150,000	25%
£250,000	ELECTRICITY

Round 14

£1,000	THE END
£2,000	METAL
£5,000	SEAT BELT
£10,000	NEW ZEALAND
£25,000	COURT
£50,000	INDIAN
£75,000	21
£100,000	VEINS
£125,000	U
£150,000	LYRICS
£250,000	SEAL

Round 15

£1,000	MARY
£2,000	ICE
£5,000	WEST
£10,000	SUGAR
£25,000	3
£50,000	APPLE
£75,000	ONYX
£100,000	Ks
£125,000	HYDROGEN
£150,000	WALK ON THE MOON
£250,000	BIRMINGHAM

Round 16

£1,000	MERCURY
£2,000	USA
£5,000	MARS AND JUPITER
£10,000	ARGENTINA
£25,000	MOUNTAINS
£50,000	PERFORMER
£75,000	180
£100,000	TAIWAN
£125,000	11
£150,000	STATUE
£250,000	ROYAL ARMOURIES

Round 17

£1,000	2
£2,000	NOVEMBER
£5,000	SIAMESE
£10,000	USA
£25,000	GRAVITY
£50,000	TORONTO
£75,000	VENUS
£100,000	NEWTON
£125,000	HYPHEN
£150,000	IRON
£250,000	PLAYING

Round 18

£1,000	ALL OF THEM
£2,000	EINE
£5,000	IRISH
£10,000	RHYME
£25,000	RICHARD I
£50,000	HAPPY
£75,000	AFRICA
£100,000	TOWNS
£125,000	ALGONGUIN
£150,000	CONSTITUENCY
£250,000	COSMONAUT

Round 19

£1,000	ENGLAND
£2,000	EUROPE
£5,000	7
£10,000	TRIANGULAR
£25,000	GRAMS
£50,000	YELLOW
£75,000	IRIS
£100,000	6 PEARS
£125,000	SOUND
£150,000	6/10
£250,000	AUSTRALIA

Round 20

£1,000	CONTINENTS
£2,000	CAT
£5,000	LUNGS
£10,000	WOOD
£25,000	ANTHONY
£50,000	SUNDERLAND
£75,000	MEXICO CITY
£100,000	VERTEBRATES
£125,000	20:40
£150,000	15th
£250,000	EROSION

Round 21

£1,000	WOODBLOCK
£2,000	SUNDAY
£5,000	MUSIC
£10,000	PEAS
£25,000	PARABLE
£50,000	ELECTION
£75,000	CANDLE
£100,000	GARLIC
£125,000	ADVERBIAL
£150,000	PEGASUS
£250,000	CAIRO

Round 22

£1,000	FRANCE
£2,000	SCOTLAND
£5,000	WATER
£10,000	MOI
£25,000	18
£50,000	COAL
£75,000	NAZI
£100,000	Y
£125,000	0.003
£150,000	BROTHER AND SISTER
£250,000	CHARITY

Round 23

£1,000	AFRICA
£2,000	MATILDA
£5,000	EAU
£10,000	IVY
£25,000	CRIMEAN
£50,000	ALTO
£75,000	BATTLEFIELD
£100,000	PAH
£125,000	BATTERY
£150,000	NEPTUNE
£250,000	ANNO DOMINI

Round 24

£1,000	THE LORD'S PRAYER
£2,000	PLASTIC
£5,000	A BRICK
£10,000	ROMAN
£25,000	Y
£50,000	DANUBE
£75,000	URANUS
£100,000	KARMA
£125,000	FROG
£150,000	SAINT-SAENS
£250,000	JODRELL BANK

ANSWERS

Round 25

£1,000	BLACK AND WHITE
£2,000	8
£5,000	DIAMOND
£10,000	GREY
£25,000	PISA
£50,000	SUSPECT
£75,000	LAH
£100,000	4
£125,000	K
£150,000	CHARLES I
£250,000	SPAIN

Round 26

£1,000	THEY REPEL
£2,000	TOMATO KETCHUP
£5,000	<
£10,000	COUNTY
£25,000	1970s
£50,000	BICEP
£75,000	HOUSES OF PARLIAMENT
£100,000	THATCHED
£125,000	VERY GOOD
£150,000	METAPHOR
£250,000	UNITED STATES

Round 27

£1,000	JEAN
£2,000	FULL STOP
£5,000	TUDOR
£10,000	TAY
£25,000	TASMAN
£50,000	SOPRANO
£75,000	ROMANS
£100,000	360
£125,000	WERGILD
£150,000	LA MANCHE
£250,000	1/4

Round 28

£1,000	FRANCE
£2,000	CHRISTIANITY
£5,000	THIGH
£10,000	METAL
£25,000	MERCURY
£50,000	HOMME
£75,000	WHEELS
£100,000	LANCASTER
£125,000	NATIONAL PARK
£150,000	AXIS
£250,000	1/4

Round 29

£1,000	PUPPY
£2,000	AUSTRALIA
£5,000	C
£10,000	£25
£25,000	ANDREW
£50,000	SEPTEMBER
£75,000	VENUS
£100,000	LOTUS
£125,000	SHELL
£150,000	GALAXY
£250,000	MELODY

Round 30

£1,000	BONE
£2,000	AN ICEBERG
£5,000	ONIONS
£10,000	VIOLINISTS
£25,000	GUILLOTINE
£50,000	LONG AND SHORT
£75,000	SETT
£100,000	ALLITERATION
£125,000	BURNED CREAM
£150,000	JERUSALEM
£250,000	CENSUS

Round 31

£1,000	60
£2,000	CD PLAYER
£5,000	TEMPO
£10,000	SIX
£25,000	7
£50,000	CHEESE
£75,000	-8
£100,000	GATEAU
£125,000	5
£150,000	HAWK
£250,000	SAUL

Round 32

£1,000	HOLY TRINITY
£2,000	MACHETE
£5,000	CLEOPATRA
£10,000	DAVID
£25,000	COLONEL
£50,000	USA
£75,000	LAS
£100,000	YOUTH HOSTEL
£125,000	EVOLUTION
£150,000	ALBERTA
£250,000	TOTS TV

Round 33

£1,000	M
£2,000	TOOTHPASTE
£5,000	OXYGEN
£10,000	PUT YOUR ARM OUT
£25,000	CRESCENT
£50,000	07
£75,000	LIVE IN IT
£100,000	BACKBONE
£125,000	QUAKERS
£150,000	NIAGARA
£250,000	3

Round 34

£1,000	16
£2,000	PYRAMIDS
£5,000	FLORENCE NIGHTINGALE
£10,000	TRANSPARENT
£25,000	CELERY
£50,000	PEACE BE UPON HIM
£75,000	GREEN
£100,000	X
£125,000	REPAIR
£150,000	CONCRETE
£250,000	STRAITJACKET

Round 35

£1,000	THE AIR
£2,000	MOSQUE
£5,000	ALPHABETICAL
£10,000	PSALMS
£25,000	DO YOU SPEAK FRENCH?
£50,000	FOB
£75,000	TELESCOPE
£100,000	YEAST
£125,000	EDMOND
£150,000	BRISTOL
£250,000	LAIKA

Round 36

£1,000	LOUIS
£2,000	CROQUET
£5,000	FRANCE
£10,000	20
£25,000	CANCER
£50,000	BRAHMAN
£75,000	VICTORIA
£100,000	DIAL
£125,000	ALASKA
£150,000	FRANCE
£250,000	DIJON

Round 37

£1,000	5
£2,000	GERMANY
£5,000	BOOKS
£10,000	TADPOLE
£25,000	END OF A WORD
£50,000	SHOOTING STAR
£75,000	SLIEVE DONARD
£100,000	CORNWALL
£125,000	REBECCA
£150,000	TOAST
£250,000	WHITE

Round 38

£1,000	JASON
£2,000	MOUSE
£5,000	FRIDAY
£10,000	NEPTUNE
£25,000	TURKEY
£50,000	ITALY
£75,000	MONASTERIES
£100,000	CELLO
£125,000	MINERS' LAMP
£150,000	RED
£250,000	WILLIAM WILBERFORCE

Round 39

£1,000	CALF
£2,000	508
£5,000	2
£10,000	QUARTER TO SEVEN
£25,000	PHILIP
£50,000	DIWALI
£75,000	49 CM^2
£100,000	16th
£125,000	THANES
£150,000	BEAT
£250,000	TEMPLE

Round 40

£1,000	SANDWICH
£2,000	LIBRARY
£5,000	CHARIOT RACING
£10,000	LIFE JACKET
£25,000	AFRICA
£50,000	48p
£75,000	SOPRANINO
£100,000	WINSTON CHURCHILL
£125,000	VOLT
£150,000	BANANA
£250,000	BARCELONA

Round 41

£1,000	5p
£2,000	NEPTUNE
£5,000	EAT IT
£10,000	FLEET OF SHIPS
£25,000	8
£50,000	£5
£75,000	THEIR RIGHTS
£100,000	AUSTRALIA
£125,000	PAVAROTTI
£150,000	ENGLAND
£250,000	WHEAT